How to Generate Values in Young Children

Foreword by Nancy Stone
Illustrations by Kathy Jones
Graphics by Patrick G. Hager

How to Generate Values in Young Children

Integrity
Honesty
Individuality
Self-Confidence
and Wisdom

by Sue Spayth Riley

The New South Company
924 Westwood Boulevard, Suite 935
Los Angeles, CA 90024

First Published 1979
Third Printing 1980

Distributed by Persea Books, Inc.
225 Lafayette Street, New York, N.Y. 10012

The quotation from "Some Reflections on the Value of Children's Play" by Sue Spayth Riley is reprinted by permission from *Young Children*, Vol. 28, No. 3 (Feb. 1973), p. 146. Copyright © 1973, National Association for the Education of Young Children, 1834 Connecticut Avenue, N.W., Washington, DC 20009.

The quotation from *Personal Growth* by Clark Moustakas is reprinted by permission from the publisher, Howard A. Doyle Publishing Co., Cambridge, MA 02139.

The quotation from "Messing Around in Science" by David Hawkins is reprinted by permission from *Science and Children*, Vol. 2, No. 5 (Feb. 1965), p. 6.

also by The New South Company

White Trash, an anthology
of contemporary Southern poets

Bear Crossings, an anthology
of North American Poets

to THOMAS, JEREMIAH, MICHAEL,
and JESSE

Contents

Acknowledgments

There are several special people who have given me help and encouragement in writing this book: Elizabeth Rosenthal who first urged me to attempt its publication; Debby Allen, whose perceptive comments from the vantage point of a young mother were invaluable; Naomi Myles and Joanne Fortune, fellow writers who stood by me in the days of solitary effort.

Alice Thompson, a long-time colleague in the classroom has shared insights with me and has provided the opportunity for lengthy dialogue, both of which have gone a long way toward the clarification of my own educational philosophy.

Nancy Stone of the New South Company has added the astute editorial assistance that has helped make this book better than it otherwise would have been. And, finally, for patience, wise comment, and much proofreading time, thanks are due my husband, Jesse, and our youngest son, Michael.

To all those children I've taught and their parents from whom I've learned so much, I have more gratitude than can be expressed.

Foreword

This is a book about the pursuit of happiness in a free society. It assumes that the essential means in the pursuit are the ability to make intelligent choices among alternatives, to make decisions that are logical and compatible, and to be confidently creative.

In this book Sue Spayth Riley acknowledges the factors and complexities of modern life which inhibit the development of values in children while stating that we need not surrender to them.

Children who enter adulthood without experience in the process of choosing, deciding, and being creative are handicapped. Their chances for success in life are diminished. In a sense, they are a burden to themselves. Very often, they also become a burden to society. Instead of developing values in which they believe, they respond to force, fear, and greed, and find at best a life of dullness and frustration.

Moral and ethical values are imperative to happiness. They arise from choices between modes of conduct and a decision to follow one or another. Confidence in one's ability to derive satisfaction from a particular set of values stems from the experiences one gains in self-generated activities in work, education, or recreation during which such choices occur. The essences and processes of choosing, deciding, and being creative not only form the roots of each individual's set of values, but also taken together generate the value structure of our entire society.

Although there are parents and teachers who understand the need to give children confidence and skill in choosing, decision making, and creative works, many need to know how to accomplish that purpose. It is hoped that *How To Generate Values in Young Children* offers insight and a simple methodology for beginning the most valuable process which young children can to generate their life's values.

Mrs. Riley's observations of young children over more than thirty years have proven to her that when you give boys and girls the freedom to evaluate, decide, create, and re-create their world, they usually construct a happy place, a place with meaning that expresses truths and dreams that are very real to them.

When children interpret those meanings and truths, and select priorities, and finally make efforts to change—freely and frequently—what does not satisfy them, they generate within themselves an inspiring force that they feel in the form of confidence and a positive attitude about their lives which any parent or teacher can see as the children work and play.

The following is an excerpt from a history of the Ferrer Modern School which Mrs. Riley is preparing. It illustrates, in part, the roots of her conviction and inspiration in the guidance of the ethical and moral education of young children.

> The school building was one low-slung story, situated at the bend of a dirt road on the crown of a softly rolling hill. At least, in the flat lands of New Jersey it could be called a hill. The building, small for a school, was covered with stucco of a nondescript brown. A wide porch extended half way across the face of it, giving a

view of the road and beyond that, the Ferrer Colony, a community of several hundred persons. The dirt road, dubbed School Street, but with no markings as such, meandered down the hill, across the brook, and led in a mile or so to the highway and the outside civilization of Piscataway Township; to the west, New Market and on to the Watchung Hills; to the east, Stelton, New Brunswick, and the Atlantic coastline.

From the schoolhouse porch could be seen scattered dwellings, some larger than the school, some smaller, all of different shapes and designs reflecting the individuality of those who built them. Most were weather-beaten and in disrepair; some were so small they were little more than shacks. Tarpaper covering was the most unifying building material of this unorthodox assortment. Near the brook the growth of trees and underbrush was thick; otherwise, the land was open to the sun; flat and muddy during the spring thaw, caked in summer's heat.

To the rear of the main schoolhouse were several smaller buildings, one housing the print and woodworking shops, a second, The Kropotkin Library, where in days gone by white-bearded Hippolyte Havel and his anarchist cronies gathered each evening to reaffirm their philosophies and re-argue world politics. As a school child in those early days, I have no recollection of ever seeing Hippolyte during the daytime when the school swarmed with boys and girls, but when by chance I happened to be out at night I could see this group through the windows of the library. Their faces aglow in the lamplight were animated with thought as they gestured excitedly, rehashing the old isms, living Laurence Veysey's observation that "agressive contention was a

shared value . . . in contrast to a culture where it is con-
sidered important to hold one's feelings in." As a child I
don't think I was impressed by Hippolyte's opinions
(for I'm sure I did not understand them) but I was much
taken with the large belly that ballooned beneath his
white, Russian smock.

A third structure, used to house some members of
the school faculty, stood beside the Kropotkin Library.
Beyond it were woods where one could always collect
hickory nuts in the fall. And farther still, on land that
had been fertile truck farms was the sprawl of Camp
Kilmer, the World War II Embarkation Center, de-
serted, but soon to become the distribution center for
refugees of the Hungarian Revolution.

On a Saturday afternoon in the fall of 1952, there
were no children around the school. The Kropotkin Library was empty; Hippolyte Havel was long since dead.
The roof over the porch of the school building resem-
bled a half-lowered eyelid in a dozing face, the face of
an old man dreaming of his youth, nodding in the warm
autumn sunshine. Built in 1920 by the unskilled hands
of the early colonists, the building was about to end its
life on earth, for within a year it was to be closed as a
school, and in 1955 leveled to the ground by the ravages
of fire.

But that time had not yet come. A small group in
serious discussion was gathered around a table in one of
the classrooms. The tone of the conversation was quiet,
and though not exactly weary it was subdued and
thoughtful. Those present were with a few exceptions
in their fifties and sixties. In keeping with the building,
their attitudes had taken on the retrospective mellow-

ness of later years. I remained to the side. I was, as a young adult, a new addition to the group, one of the final boards of the Ferrer Modern School. The talk I heard that quiet Saturday afternoon was in distinct contrast to the loud, explosive, and lengthy discussions I remembered overhearing as a child.

The two other young people present were a couple recently hired to take over the school in a last-ditch effort to revive what had been since 1911 one of the most viable and creative experiments in progressive education in this country during the time when the progressive movement was at its height. Though the Modern School developed and grew from the same ferment as other progressive schools, such as the Walden School, the City and Country School, and the Horace Mann School, it was different in one very important respect. It was the focal point of a rural community, a counterculture, if you will, that gave sustenance and support to the school, and received from it, vitality and commitment.

The young couple were no further into life than their early twenties; their ideas were fraught with feeling, almost bristling, in contrast to the time-softened attitudes of the older group. The young woman was especially uncompromising in the surety of her views. She held her first child, a baby of several months, in her arms. As she suckled the infant she defended her opinions. A fine-looking woman, she would have been beautiful if humorless fanaticism had not so wholly consumed her demeanor.

"When they are ready—when they see the need for using the puzzles—they'll sort them out and pick up the pieces!" The husband nodded agreement; the others shook their heads, and one, an elderly teacher in the school, a woman of warmth and experience, said,

"You're asking too much—they're young; there is too much confusion. They need guidance . . ." her voice trailed off.

With an abrupt motion that shifted the infant to the second breast, the young woman responded with intensity,

"If this is a free school, as you told us when you asked us to come here, then it is up to the children to pick up those pieces, to learn by their mistakes, to accept responsibility—to accept the consequences."

A man whose leathered face was a shade of tan that almost matched the faded brown of his work shirt, leaned across the table opposite the young woman and replied,

"But you see, this is not what we mean by *free* or by *responsibility*. This situation has become a battle of wills between you and the children." He leaned back in his chair and added, as though in summary, "Chaos is not freedom."

In a room down the hall—the playroom for the youngest children—the entire floor was littered with hundreds of wooden puzzle pieces, a discouraging heap of small, variegated shapes. The shelves where the puzzles had been stored were completely empty. The puzzles were an extensive collection of years, and usually only a few were taken down at a time. So unbounded was the freedom the young couple had given the children that their behavior had gotten out of hand to the extent that a group of them had thrown all the puzzles to the floor in a torrent of uncontrolled childish rioting. Jumbled even more by other toys and equipment, the pieces had remained there, unsorted and stepped on.

The young couple, so imbued with their hands-off philosophy of "free" education, refused to stop the rampage, or when it had wound down, to help the children regain order in their surroundings. Initially, these teachers had either been unable or unwilling to provide an appropriate framework for a program in which the children might have the opportunity to develop their own inner controls as well as their creativity.

Though the problem with the puzzles may seem a trivial matter, the frequency of such conflict in the thoughts and philosophy of libertarian or progressive education is significant. As I research the beginnings of the Modern School at Stelton and as I study the current educational scene—the mushrooming of "free" schools and the development of "open" education in and out of the public school system—it is clear that there is danger in a simplistic interpretation of the meaning of freedom. The recognition of the complexity of the idea of freedom with its accompanying responsibility is of profound importance and must join with an ability to relate the two to a definition of the teacher's role and to the nature of a curriculum.

Within a month the young couple had moved on, leaving the small house to the rear vacant for another teacher, Myron Jacobson, who came to try out his ideas in the aging stucco schoolhouse. Jacobson had none of the fanaticism of the previous pair. His intelligence, warmth, and humor kept him there for many months working with the several elderly teachers remaining from past times, but by then it was too late. Attendance had dwindled, and most of the children were of preschool age. The community which had supported the school was fast decaying. Moving into the homes were a conglomerate of poor from the urban center of New Brunswick and middle-class families from other areas who sought housing during a time when housing was scarce. The colony was becoming just another neighborhood of the metropolitan sprawl. Few who moved in cared or even knew about the school.

In 1953, the doors were regretfully, but with finality, closed. The building was put on the market, the windows boarded against vandalism, and all records were turned over to the archives at Rutgers University. "Not with a bang but a whimper" did a living memorial to the martyred Francisco Ferrer, the Spanish educator who was killed in 1909, pass into history.

I doubt that Sue Spayth Riley's remarkable educational experiences could be duplicated in the 1970s. Her childhood was dominated by the Ferrer Modern School in Stelton, New Jersey. Her undergraduate years were spent studying drama in North Carolina at Black Mountain College, that infamous and famous experiment in community. She later received a degree in early childhood education at Goddard College in Plainfield, Vermont, through Goddard's innovative alternate adult program.

Sue Spayth's own early childhood was marked by frequent moves and many periods of poverty, but the move to the Ferrer Colony with her parents and younger brother in 1929 began a period of stability during the Great Depression when most of the rest of the country was in great disruption. The stability did not stem from prosperity or material goods, for the several hundred people who made up the colony were largely unemployed—the first to be affected by hard times—and were casting about for ways to survive. Although the colony was rural and very poor, it was inhabited primarily by philosophical anarchists who were peaceful, intelligent characters of very diverse backgrounds, and the entire community centered around the Ferrer Modern School. Her parents, who had both worked for newspapers, started their own paper in nearby Dunellen, New Jersey, and the Spayths eventually moved from the colony, but remained in the area for many years.

After finishing high school in Dunellen, Sue Spayth entered Black Mountain College, where she met and married Jeremiah Wolpert, a philosophy student, in 1942. During the war, she was a reporter for the Hays, Kansas, *Daily News*. In the first years after the war, she was employed at Time, Inc. in New York. When her husband died suddenly of polio, she returned to Dunellen with her two small boys and went to work as the news editor of her father's paper. She also participated in a cooperative nursery school, and this was her first formal training in early childhood education.

In 1958, she married Jesse Riley, a scientist with Celanese Corporation. A son was born, and soon after, the Rileys moved to Charlotte, North Carolina, where Sue Spayth Riley realized her dream of a school for all children. Of the time she spent at the Ferrer Modern School, Mrs. Riley says, "I learned there a deep sense of respect for the differences in people and for the development of humanitarian values." These were the qualities she brought to the Open Door School.

The Open Door School, begun in 1966 under the sponsorship of the Unitarian Church of Charlotte, was the first weekday preschool in Charlotte to actively recruit children from all representative economic levels, religions, and races. It served as a workshop in nonsectarian education and a viable example of integration in a divided city. Mrs. Riley and the teachers at the Open Door School worked with parents and community organizations to urge other preschools to provide scholarships and to admit the children of minorities. When court-ordered integration came into effect in Charlotte in 1970, many of the privately-held and church-sponsored preschools had followed the lead of the Open Door School in preparing children for a balance between their lives and their educations.

Today, Sue Spayth Riley, with a graduate degree from The University of North Carolina, continues as an advisor to the Open Door School and the Council that directs it. At the request of various institutions, she conducts workshops in early childhood education for teachers. And much of her time is spent writing about how to help young children develop their ability to learn wisdom, patience, integrity, and self-confidence.

Nancy Stone

How to Generate Values in Young Children

Bubble Gum
In The
Garden
Of Eden

Chapter 1

Learning from choosing: to achieve a reliable sense
of right and wrong, children must make choices; it
is the task of parents to make this possible.

RANDY had just turned five. His parents had promised that
after his birthday he would be old enough to have an allowance. He was delighted. Each Saturday he was to have fifty cents
to spend as he wished.

Early the very first Saturday morning, Randy and his father
took off for the local variety store. Randy, the two quarters jumping merrily together in his pocket, walked tall with the determination of new responsibility.

In the store Randy thoughtfully surveyed the toy counter,
examining, discussing, asking occasionally for some help with
prices. The selection was limited because so many handsome little
cars and other items were priced well beyond his budget. There
were a few plastic cars for forty-eight cents, but Randy properly
characterized them as "crummy." The bright balls of bubble gum,
each separately wrapped, were two cents each. With fifty cents,
he calculated, he could buy a feast—twenty-five pieces. A whole
bag full! Never before had he had more than one piece at a time.
Then there were some toy pistols for thirty-nine cents and some
books for forty-nine.

It was difficult to decide, but Randy savored the indecision
and his authority. His father, who was thinking about the lawn

that needed mowing and the dirty car that needed washing, became impatient.

"What about this little fire engine, or this book?" his father said.

"No, the fire engine has crooked wheels, and I don't want a book."

"Well, how about this paint set?"

"Naw, that's baby stuff."

"Hurry up, Randy." His father's voice had an edge to it. "Why not decide on the book or the fire engine?"

After a short pause, a thoughtful one. Randy said, "Okay, I think I've decided."

"Good," said his father with obvious relief.

"I'm going to buy twenty-five pieces of bubble gum, all colors except purple." His father frowned.

"Not bubble gum. It's bad for your teeth, and besides it will be all gone in a day."

"But I want the bubble gum. I'll get more of it than anything else. I've decided."

"No! No bubble gum."

"Okay," said Randy, accepting his father's denial, "then I'll look around some more." He wandered off. Finally he spotted a nifty little water pistol for fifty cents.

"Hey, I'll get this, Daddy." Daddy examined it carefully.

"Randy, this won't hold up for an hour. It's cheap. Why don't you save your money until next week then you'll have a dollar and can buy a better water pistol."

"But Daddy, I want to spend my allowance *now*, and I really do want the bubble gum. And besides you said I could decide . . ." his voice trailed off. "Please, Daddy!"

"Now Randy, bubble gum isn't a good thing to buy with your allowance. It's just junk . . ."

And so ran the dialogue between Randy and his father. Finally, Randy decided on the fire engine with rickety wheels that he really did not want very much, and his father allowed him to spend the remaining two cents on a piece of red bubble gum. They left the store. Relieved to have the ordeal over, Daddy resolved to turn the shopping trip over to Mother next week.

Though he was unaware of the implications of his father's interference with his choices, Randy was being cheated. Daddy had inadvertently deprived his son of a valuable learning experience. Daddy had also broken a promise: he had given Randy an area of choice, but then had thoughtlessly proceeded to hem him in with restrictions. Daddy's opinions based on *his* experience may have been correct—bubble gum is bad for your teeth and a cheap water pistol will soon break. But these are things for Randy to learn for himself, not from Daddy.

Adults, having learned so much from long experience, often find it difficult to give children defined areas of choice and then stand back and allow them to use their freedom. "Oops, he's making a mistake" comes so easily that it is hard for Daddy not to insist that he knows best, for of course he usually does. Yet the parents' knowledge cannot be spoon-fed to the children. One of the major responsibilities of adults is to give children freedom to learn from their own experiences and to shoulder the consequences of their choices. Too often we are inclined to isolate the virtue of responsibility and assume it can be taught in a vacuum. We say to ourselves, "The chores must be done each morning so my child will learn to be responsible." We need to realize that freedom and responsibility are inseparable, and that one cannot be learned without the other.

The bubble gum episode may seem inconsequential, but when it is added to many more such episodes in the life of a small child, it could retard the child's ability to explore alternatives, examine consequences, study all sides of a question, and make a decision. The child, let us say a boy like Randy, may grow into the kind of adult who will easily turn important moral decisions over to whatever authority is available and blindly follow the established patterns of others, regardless of their merit. Whether he develops into a submissive and conformist individual is certainly not going to depend upon whether or not his father allowed him the purchase of twenty-five pieces of bubble gum when he was five years old. It does appear, however, that the accumulation of such experiences will influence the development of his character.

I have observed that in raising children some parents think of decision making only in very lofty terms. For them, decisions are grandiose choices between earth-shaking alternatives and may be turned over to children only when they have reached the age of reason. It is quite true that earth-shaking moral decisions cannot and should not be presented to young children. The opportunity, however, to make decisions involving less significant options may be given to the very young. Practice in the *process* of choosing is a must, with the options being in keeping with the age and ability of each child. When children are given practice in choosing, the chances are good that they will develop decision-making ability, insight, flexibility, and the imagination to cope with the loftier choices to come later.

At five, choices may involve bubble gum and water pistols. Later alternatives will almost certainly concern an occupation, a spouse, a vote for a president, a war, a cause. Human beings possess the capacity to symbolize, to reason, to imagine; we have a sense of time, an ability to project our thoughts into the future, and to calculate the results of our choices two weeks or two years ahead. We are born with the capacity to be sensitive to others and to contemplate the possible effects of our decisions. Decisions, large and small, are the responsibility of the human species; we are "condemned" to freedom and to the responsibility that goes with it. Choices given other species are limited by instinctual drives. The human being is the only one with this glorious, albeit sobering, condemnation.

The awesomeness of the unique human capacity to choose is expressed symbolically in Genesis. Before Adam and Eve stole the forbidden fruit they were innocent, unseeking, unquestioning, and safe in Eden where God's authority ruled. All this changed when Eve picked the fruit, persuaded by the serpent who promised, "When you eat of it your eyes will be opened and you will be like God, knowing good and evil." Suddenly, they were thrown on their own with the full knowledge of their potential as human beings.

HUMAN childhood is relatively longer than that of most other species. When you come to think of it, growing up takes about one quarter or more of our entire life span. There is much to absorb and accomplish during these first several decades of life— a complex and interrelated mass of physical, emotional, intellectual, and social learnings that cannot be separated and isolated for teaching one at a time. Our parental responsibility toward the young accordingly spans a good portion of our adulthood and is significantly more intricate and challenging than the assignment of parenthood given the wolf, the cat, or the chicken. Since we human beings are the only species with the ability to make choices, to plan ahead, to reason, to carve out values, it must follow that the human faculty we need most importantly to encourage in our young is the ability to choose. We must provide the child with a rich variety of opportunities for decision making—based, of course, upon the child's age and willingness to accept and profit by the responsibilities that go with the decisions.

To neglect to nurture the gifts of choosing as we raise our children invites ruinous consequences. Yet too often, without meaning to, we are guilty of neglect. We surround children with rules, regulations, and prohibitions. We hand them values ready-made, we lecture, we moralize, we stuff them with facts. Then when they reach adulthood, we assume the success of our training, and as they step out into the world we say in effect, "Run along now. I've given you all I can. Make your own decisions, fend for yourself, be self-reliant, and Godspeed."

Areas for choice in childhood must nevertheless be carefully selected. In an excessive burst of enthusiasm for the idea of freedom, parents may be tempted to overload children with too many options. Too much freedom can be crippling to the healthy growth of a child. Burdened with more freedom than they can handle at any particular age, children may develop in one of two undesirable directions: either the disproportionate amount of freedom creates confusion and insecurity that prevents the growth of inner discipline and confidence, or it encourages a license that results in unbounded self-centered activity, willfulness and, to use the good old-fashioned term, a spoiled child. Such behavior is generally the result of complete permissiveness, though I hesitate to use the word as its meaning has become elusive, changing according to the context in which it is used. The fact remains, though, that it is a disservice to children to give them more responsibility and freedom than they can handle at any given age.

To determine how much freedom and which choices to give a child is often baffling. For this is our area of choice, and the task is not an easy one. But we should be able to provide a sensible balance between too much and too little freedom if we maintain a certain objectivity. We must be wary of the danger of becoming bossy—an easy posture when our primary concern is the preservation of our ego rather than the child's development. At the same time we must not risk the abdication of our control by an anything-goes attitude.

As far as I can determine there is no precise formula that we can use. However, *our* decisions about *children's* decisions will be best if we can develop a kind of sensitivity to age, an openness to needs, and awareness of the dynamics of growth and of the way children respond to and use freedom.

RANDY's father was impatient. He was not sensitive to his son's thoughtful attitude toward a new responsibility and his pride in assuming it. He did not understand Randy's five-year-old appreciation of quantity and his really fine mathematical ability. Furthermore, having promised something and then taken it away, he was not honest with Randy. If for some specific reason bubble gum was forbidden, he should have made that clear beforehand. "You may spend the fifty cents any way you like or save it if you wish, but you may not buy gum or candy." Randy would have accepted this and most probably worked happily within the prescribed boundaries.

Though often inadvertent, adult dishonesty involving decision making appears in many forms. There are those who seem to be giving children several options, but distort the freedom by conspicuously hoping they will choose the option the parents believe to be best. If the children choose the other way, the parents will attempt to change their minds by wheedling, persuading, arguing. This is a kind of manipulation that results in nothing but resentment and guilt in the children. Their decisions are either theirs or not. When a youngster asks to go to the movies during the week and you are opposed to it, it is much better to say simply, "Sorry, Son, I know you want to go, but tonight you may not," rather than opening the door to argument by, "Why do you want to go tonight? You'll be awfully sleepy in school tomorrow. Besides . . ." Another type of dishonesty is obvious when the parent gives the child a choice but loads it with warnings and advice. If the child, let us say Randy again, does not heed the advice, but buys the toy that breaks and Daddy is on the scene to say, "I told you so," Randy has not had the freedom to learn from a mistake, because now his mistake is all mixed up with feelings of irritation and resentment. If he accepts Daddy's advice and passes up the toy that may break, though it is the one he really wanted, he is going to feel he had been pressured and is less his own person.

THERE are many areas in which teachers and parents may give the freedom to decide, without qualm that the choices will be upsetting—areas in which one or the other decision should not make a whit of difference to the adult, but which may be very meaningful to children. The choosing of clothing is a fine example of an opportunity often neglected, perhaps because parents sometimes think less of their children as unique individuals and more of them as extensions of the parents' images. What children wear is very much a part of how they feel at a particular time and how they feel about themselves. Clothing is an expression of the development of their selfhood and identity. (We have the same feelings about our clothes, don't we?) Within reasonable limits the choice of clothing is an area of determination that parents should turn over to their offspring.

One chilly spring morning Emily, a young-four-year old in my nursery school class, came in looking very pleased with herself. "Hey, Mrs. Riley, look!" She pulled up her shirt and pushed down her pants to show me that beneath these winter-type clothes she had on her bathing suit. "See, I wore my bathing suit *under* my clothes, 'cause Mamma said it was too cold to wear my bathing suit, and it is *almost* summer, but not summer yet." Emily was delighted with her creative solution to the impasse with her mother that morning. Her mother was one who allowed her daughter considerable leeway in clothing choices, and it showed in the charming heterogeneous combinations Emily wore. That morning Mother had obviously put her foot down about the bathing suit. To wear the double set of clothes was Emily's solution. Fortunately, her wise mother was less concerned about being boss than making sure her daughter was warm on a raw spring day. Otherwise, their disagreement could easily have become a battle of wills. As it was, Emily had a happy morning and grew a little more toward fulfillment of herself as an independent and imaginative person. Compare another child's ruined morning.

Peter was also four. He was a shy child who was having difficulty leaving his mother. After several weeks, though, he was feeling more secure in class and was beginning to participate. One morning his mother, obviously distraught, poked her head in the door and asked for my help with Peter. She had been persuading and coaxing him in the hall, but Peter would not come in. I found Peter stiff against the wall, uncommunicative and angry. I noticed he was wearing a handsome, hand-knit sweater. After talking with him for several minutes, I suggested to his mother that she leave. She did, and Peter made no move to detain her. Finally he came in, but spent most of the morning glum, resentful, and quiet. I could not determine what the trouble had been though obviously he and his mother had had some sort of set-to. It was a wasted morning for the child. He was unable to let go, to do anything. He seemed to have lost the slowly won gains of the past weeks of adjustment. Later I discovered that he and his mother had had a battle about wearing the sweater. He had wanted to wear something else, and for a reason I cannot remember, she had insisted on the new sweater.

A sweater, some bubble gum—small things in themselves— are to a young child tremendously vital and represent areas in which he or she should be allowed to exercise judgment, express feelings and a sense of self. By respecting children's choices in such matters we are respecting their dignity and their ability to choose. When we jump in with "teaching" in mind or "mother knows best" or just simply to prove that we are in charge, our attitude as well as our actions are a sharp slap to emerging selfhood. If we can remember that *it is the process of choosing that counts* and not get hung up on the particular choices children make, then I think we are on the right track. When we fuss with children over choices in such matters as clothes or dime store purchases the significance of the controversy goes beyond new sweaters or bubble gum. Rather, it attacks the very core of identity and self-respect.

When children choose for themselves they experience the authority of self-determination.

As children grow the quality of alternatives will change and their decisions will involve matters more weighty to the adult eye. If they are schooled in the process their chances of choosing wisely are better. A touching example is found in a story told me by a friend concerning her seventeen-year-old son. This mother is staunchly committed to allowing her children as many opportunities as possible for making decisions, and she has practiced this philosophy since her children were very young.

Harry had become attracted to his best friend's girl, but had kept hands off. He had discussed this with his mother and revealed how deeply he felt about the girl and how difficult it was to stay away from her, although he believed it would be wrong to do otherwise. The mother had sympathized and agreed that he was doing the right thing. The best friend became very ill and was sent to a hospital hundreds of miles away. Harry stuck to his decision until the best friend had been gone for some months. Then, coming to the conclusion that he had kept away long enough, he began to date the girl.

One evening Harry was on the kitchen telephone speaking in low, serious tones. Quite accidentally, the mother overheard him say, "I just feel terribly guilty, that's all—it isn't right and I don't feel right about it at all." The mother told me she fled to the front of the house not wishing to eavesdrop. She assumed he was talking to the girl, and her mind raced fearfully to conclusions concerning the reason for his guilt. She said nothing during the subsequent days, nor did her son. It soon became evident that the two young people had broken up. After the first sadness had passed, Harry seemed happier, less abstracted and more himself than he had been for a long time. Finally, he told his mother about it, explaining that he could not continue dating his best friend's

15

girl, even though the best friend was far away. The relationship had been further complicated by the fact that the girl had not officially broken with the other boy. "And it's just *that* that made it worse, Mother," he explained. "I was taking advantage of them both. It was a hard decision, but I feel right about it now."

In his book, *Personal Growth*, Clark Moustakas says that the "challenge of authentic choice is a real challenge today because the values of the school and society are, in many respects, geared to successful achievement and a high place in the social hierarchy." It is more difficult than ever for young adults to make choices based upon values of justice and respect for human dignity when these values are in conflict with the materialism and opportunism in our culture. The young must often make their choices alone. If they are to have the strength, the insight, and the self-confidence to choose fairness over expediency, it is imperative that we nurture their ability to choose courageously and wisely just as carefully as we nurture their bodies.

When a child, a girl for example, is pushed, prodded, directed, and confined from a very young age and is thought of primarily as a product of the teachings of parents and school and when she is turned off and repulsed in the pursuits that are meaningful and exhilarating to her, she becomes alienated from herself and distrustful of her intuitions and affirmations. She learns to fit herself into the molds of society. When she becomes an adult, she may feel a stirring in the deepest recesses of her soul and know that something is wrong with her personal world. But such stirrings will serve only to make her fearful, and she will confine her anxieties by continuing to settle for the security of society's prevailing patterns.

Personal values and the gift of making choices compatible with those values develop slowly from within. Such values do not come from injections by persons in authority or by superficially copying society's patterns. They must be searched for, tried out, discussed and analyzed. Alternatives must be scrutinized and weighed. Every available resource of the human mind and heart must be activated. To achieve a reliable sense of right and wrong, children must exercise their human potential. They must make choices. It is the task of parents to make this possible.

The Crumbs
From The
Wood
After The Saw
Sawed It

Chapter 2

Learning from seeing, touching, experiencing: to interpret reality, children must experience their surroundings through imagination and discovery.

PARENTS, even those who are apprehensive about losing control, are often surprised to discover the many decision-making experiences they may make available to children without risk. Initial parental fears are certainly understandable. None of us wants to throw children into a complex and frightening situation beyond their ability to manage. Neither do we want to neglect our parental responsibilities of leadership, guidance, and counsel. There are, however, many ways in which we can open the doors to more freedom and responsibility, ways that are legitimate and appropriate for the children, *and* comfortable for the parents. Often, we are not aware of these decision-making areas, because they appear so insignificant.

When children explore their world through play with materials, toys, and friends, using their imagination to interpret reality and to discover themselves in relation to their environment, they are confronting opportunities in abundance for the free use of initiative, judgment, and choosing. When drawing, painting, or working with materials such as wood or clay, children may be —and should be—given a maximum of freedom to make decisions without adult interference.

Parents can learn a great deal by visiting a good nursery school or kindergarten and observing teachers interacting with children as they work and play.

Susie enters her nursery school class. After hanging up her coat she goes directly to the table where collage materials and paste have been put out. The many choices she will make during the morning begin with her decision to paste rather than play with blocks, dolls, or any of the many other activities provided. She picks a large, green piece of construction paper; then from a variety of smaller, assorted shapes of different colors, she chooses several and pastes them on the green paper—quite freely, with no directions from the teacher. After placing three pieces on the background sheet she is finished. The teacher expresses interest in her work, comments on her choice of shapes, and writes her name in the corner.

Susie is satisfied; this is entirely her work. If the teacher had even suggested, no matter how sweetly, that she fill up the empty places with more shapes, Susie would have doubted her own judgment. If the teacher had asked her, "What is it?" Susie might have responded with a shrug at such a foolish question or with defensiveness at what she perceived as a criticism. The collage was an expression of how she felt at the time and was not supposed to *be* anything. If Susie had done something representational, the teacher might have given her the opportunity to identify it by asking, "Would you like to tell me about your collage, Susie?" With this open approach Susie would neither have felt compelled to describe it, if she had had something definite in mind, nor would she have been put in the position of degrading her own work by admitting to the teacher, "Isn't nothin'." Susie would have been free to tell or not to tell. The decision would have been hers.

Then Johnny comes to the table. With much dash and enthusiasm he pastes and pastes and pastes, shape after shape after shape. Soon his entire paper is covered, some pieces overlapping, several sticking out over the edge. Whereas Susie worked slowly, thoughtfully, and chose only three pieces, Johnny, for reasons expressive of the essence of his unique being, piles on and on. When he finishes he covers the whole conglomerate with a liberal layer of extra paste. The teacher accepts and respects these differences, not only in choice, but in approach and temperament. She makes no attempt to evaluate the product. She knows that to a child it is the process that is important.

At another table painting is underway. Brad is humming as he paints, and it is obvious to the teacher that he had something in his mind before he sat down.

"Mmm," she thinks—but does not say aloud—"it looks like a house." Beside the house Brad is painting a blue figure; then a yellow sun appears at the top of the paper. The teacher is interested, but makes no comment.

In a few minutes Brad calls to her, "See, teacher, this is my house and that is my mother, the sun is really shining big. But then," muses Brad as he dips his brush in the black paint, "it starts to rain, like it did that time a long time ago. A big storm." And with verve he sweeps the brush of black across the house, the mother, the sun. In several minutes the paper is almost covered with black.

"That's an interesting story to go with your picture, Brad," responds the teacher. "I enjoyed hearing about it."

Brad grins, and says, "Okay, let's hang it up to dry." They do.

The teacher, who in no way had attempted to prevent Brad from covering the picture with black paint, feels confident that at lunch time when Brad walks in happily with the painting, his mother, whom she knows to be a wise parent, will give Brad the opportunity to tell her the story of the storm rather than commenting peremptorily, "My goodness, Brad, what a depressing picture, all black. Why didn't you paint a cheerful picture?"

LEGITIMATE choices for a young child must be scrupulously protected. When he or she works with art materials, the choices during the process must reflect his or her feelings and perceptions. Art activities are a rich source of the first important steps in the development of imagination, creativity, self-reliance, and the ability to choose between alternatives. It is frequently difficult for an adult to realize that the process is of primary concern to a child who is centered in the present and who paints, plays, and builds with a joy in improvisation, immersed in immediacy. To a young child the result of the activity is secondary. As adults our orientation and respect are for the product. With our grown-up sights directed toward results, our tendency is to provide children with patterns and directions to follow, such as cute pictures to trace.

The elementary school art teacher visiting in the classroom says, "Now children, since it's Fall, we're going to paint pretty-colored trees today. Isn't that nice?" The next day the walls of the classroom are hung with trees, all very much the same, all dotted with the identical autumn colors. (Does this reflect the public schools' espoused concern for the uniqueness of each child?) There would be no room among those trees for Brad's house and mother covered with the dynamics of the big storm.

That this is a touchy subject even to older children was made clear to me rather unexpectedly by a high school church group. I had been asked to speak to them about the Open Door School, the preschool in which I taught, and with some trepidation I said

The Crumbs From The Wood After The Saw Sawed It

I would do it, feeling sure that the last thing in the world these young people would be interested in would be early childhood education. Surprisingly, my discussion of our free choice approach to art sparked their attention and brought to the surface their own remembered feelings of anger and frustration when they were told what to draw and how to draw it; their recollections went back as far as the first and second grades. It was as though my brief introduction had served to open a Pandora's box of hurt feelings that had been smoldering for years. The whole hour was spent in a bull session, each one of them describing in detail his or her experiences with art in school. "She made me feel like *nothing!*" said Ralph, a husky high school junior, referring to the instructions from his fifth grade art teacher. "She told me my horse's legs were too short and that I should put another horse in the background." Pam recalled her acute feelings of defeat when, after spending hours happily painting a picture of her family's summer home, the teacher had asked that she paint in bricks on the wooden walls of the building she'd already laboriously reproduced.

The vivid expressions of these harbored resentments served to underline my conviction that art content and style should be off-limits to product-oriented art teachers if children are to develop confidence in their ability to make choices expressing themselves and their views of reality. In defense of art teachers, whom I really have no intention of vilifying, I will say that their emphasis upon craftsmanship and results may be valuable for older children and adults. But to a young child an art teacher's corrections or take-over of his or her picture can be a devastating experience. The high school students who told me of their feelings were mature and articulate. Younger children, when teachers or parents say, "Why don't you make the man's legs longer?" or "Stop scribbling and *draw* something," will react with just as much feeling, but will not be able to verbalize their feelings as the teenagers did.

One afternoon, Michael, our youngest son in elementary school, returned home complaining bitterly, "That silly art teacher makes me so mad. See, we had to paint a picture of a room, so my room had a yellow rug in it, and do you know what she made me do? She made me put spots on it because she said it had to be 'filled up.' Oh, she makes me so mad!" The near obsession that many art teachers have concerning the importance of covering every inch of paper is a recurring complaint. A child's concentration is on the subject of his or her personal vision. The admonition to "fill it up" comes as a rude imposition of authority.

Those who have made studies of creativity have observed that characteristics common to creative persons are: flexibility; fluency; sensitivity to problems; originality; and the ability to analyze, synthesize, and redefine materials and problems and organize them coherently. When we give a child a coloring book with directions to stay within the lines and color the pumpkin orange, are we encouraging those qualities? No, we were presenting a pattern of the worst sort and saying, in effect, "There is a right way to do it and a wrong way. You do it right." The chances are that youngsters raised on staying within the lines will fail to develop the imagination and the courage to go beyond the lines as they grow, to act independently. We fault children's thinking, choice, and judgment when we prescribe a subject or form for imitation. Though well-meant, our suggestions send to them the unspoken message, "Your choices are inadequate."

Parents can do a great deal to encourage creative activity simply by providing materials and encouraging the child's efforts. Our concern here is not with the production of a piece of art or the development of an artist. Rather, our aim is to provide the child with practice in decision making that will encourage competency in problem solving and originating—all qualities to be treasured, and ones that will be needed in abundance by the next generation if we are to maintain our humanity in a world increasingly perfunctory and ruled by technology.

Parents are often persuaded by very young children to draw *for* them. It begins innocently enough, but can become a game that is difficult to break away from. "Mommy," young Danny says, "draw me, the puppy and me." She does. He is pleased. "Now, make Daddy in the car." She does, rather enjoying it. He beams. And so on. Finally, Mommy is tired. "Okay, Son, now *you* draw." The young boy is lost, for he is not ready yet to draw representationally and even if he were he would probably feel completely inadequate, his efforts coming on the heels of the clever pictures drawn by Mommy. He is defeated before he starts. At his age he is still a scribbler and his scribbling, which had been most satisfying to him before the adult interference, will be uninteresting compared to the models his mother set before him. Scribbling should never be belittled. He must go through that stage. And it is a very important stage indeed, for it is the period in which he makes the delightful discovery that by controlling his arm and hand as his fingers hold a piece of crayon he can produce a mark on a piece of paper.

Ricky was a child in my class several years ago with a rich and searching intelligence. He had just turned five. One morning he was busy drawing a Halloween picture with crayons. He drew a witch and a jack-o-lantern, both very imaginative. Then he decided he should have a bat in the picture. He asked for help. "Now I need a bat. Mrs. Riley, will you draw the bat?"

I suspected that someone had drawn for him at some time, because children this age will hardly ever ask this unless the pattern has been initiated by an adult. "Well, no Ricky. I'm not sure about my drawing a bat for *your* picture. It's yours." I hedged, not knowing quite how to handle this as the problem rarely arises. But I did know that I was not going to draw the bat.

Ricky seemed lost but would not give up. "Please draw it. I just can't draw a bat, just can't."

"I'll tell you what," I said, "maybe we could find a picture of a bat."

He went off and left his drawing, unfinished. Later I found a book with some pictures of bats in it. He looked them over, but made no move to use that research for his own picture. I realized later that it was a mistake for me to get the book. A child that age does not draw what he *sees*, he draws what he *feels*. Besides, what I'd really done by getting the book was to give him something to copy. If I had had a real bat around to show him it might have been different for the child would then have had his own feeling reaction to it. Anyway, Ricky was unresponsive to the book, and the morning ended with no bat drawn.

He left at noon without the picture. "I don't want it."

"Shall I keep it here and hang it on the bulletin board?" I asked.

"No, throw it in the waste basket."

The next morning when he came in he immediately got out the crayons and sat down with a clean sheet of paper. He reproduced the witch and the pumpkin face of the day before, and then, as I suspected he would, he asked me to draw the bat. Anticipating this I had become very busy at the other end of the room. No one else had come in yet. With my back to him, I began, rather vaguely, "Well, Ricky, tell me what does a bat look like, and how does it act?"

"It has wings that go out this way, one on each side, and they have things going like that, and it flies," and though my back was turned I realized he had taken crayon to paper and was drawing as he talked. "And it is brownish and whooshes and sometimes scares people . . ." I turned around. "Hey, Mrs. Riley, come look at my bat."

"It's a fine bat, Ricky. I like your bat."

And then with the most delightfully, self-satisfied grin, he said, "And it's really *mine!*" He took the picture home.

Just as we allow children the freedom to make their own decisions when drawing or pasting, we must allow them freedom to discover the properties of various materials with which they may be playing or constructing. We must give them unhurried and undirected time to feel, to squish, to mash, and to absorb the information from the manipulation that their senses are sending their brains. Just as children must scribble before they draw, so must they squeeze, pat, and pound clay before producing bird's nests or pots. They must have, if they wish, time to be tentative with finger paints before plunging in up to their elbows and time to blend paints of different colors on the paper without adults badgering them.

A child like Ricky does not have to be told, "Don't mix them all together; it will turn into a sicky brown." He will find out for himself soon enough. Maybe he is simply enjoying the process of mixing, and maybe he likes the brown. And if he does not want sicky brown he will do it differently next time. He needs to be left alone to discover colors and combinations of colors for himself without the experienced adult interrupting him with instructions and teachings. "Try mixing the blue with the yellow. Then you'll make green. Just try it." He may try it and he will find out it makes green. But it would have been better to allow him the time to make the observation on his own.

At any age learning through experience sticks better. Someone can give us a lecture on how to ride a bicycle, how the brakes work, and how to balance, but we will learn best by getting on the bike, pressing the brake, falling, and learning to balance by the feel of it. The exuberant and delighted cry of a child who experiments with colors and finds that blue and yellow make green is testimony to this. Karen was painting an egg carton, trying two different colors in each small pocket. "Teacher, come look! I put in yellow, then blue on top, and look, it's getting to be green." Later, her explorations will lead to other discoveries. Pink. Orange. Purple. But not all at once. It may take weeks. The waiting though, is worth it.

Three-year-old Mary is stringing beads, thoroughly enjoying the manipulation of the bright, varicolored wooden pieces, choosing the same color twice, then another color, then a third; her tongue is between her lips in hard concentration. Not able to resist squeezing in a lesson on color identification, an inexperienced teacher asks, "Now what color is that bead, Mary?" Mary looks up, somewhat disconcerted, interrupted, "Don't know." Then, tentatively, wishing to please, "Red?" "No, that's not red. It's blue. *This* one is red." Has Mary really been taught something? Probably not. The adult's lesson was simply an interruption to Mary.

When we stand back and give children time to explore, to discover their own answers, to search for the answers even if they do not find them—there is learning in the search—we are providing fine stretches of open road for growth and decision making. And do not tell them something they have not even asked yet.

Mary was deeply involved in the bead stringing. Her chosen commitment at that moment was to practicing her fine muscle skills, matching same colors, and glorying in the sheer accumulation of beads on the string. At that time she was not a whit concerned with identifying the names of the colors.

The occasions for choosing and discovery learning when children work with wood, hammers, and nails are many. Given appropriate freedom and time with scrap wood of various shapes, sizes, textures, and grain, nails of different lengths and thicknesses, and a saw, a child will learn something of design, of mathematics, of physics. He or she will be developing flexibility and the skills of experimentation. A few simple instructions from an adult concerning the technique of using a saw and hammering a nail along with the establishment of a firm set of safety rules will suffice. After that leave the child alone. Do not cut off thinking by restricting the child to a precut, adult-imposed birdhouse project. It will be sufficient for one child to hammer a nail securely into a board, for another to nail two pieces of wood together. For a third, perhaps an older boy or girl or one who has had experience in woodworking, the project will become a treasured airplane, maybe with wings uneven, but the child's very own construction.

If we do not impose patterns children will not feel defeated by crooked wings, nor will they feel inadequate because the first nail they chose was too short to go through two small boards. They will simply try again another way, learning constantly through experimentation.

A woodworking shop in a nursery school is a microcosm packed with a vast assortment of opportunities for initiative and problem solving. One morning Debbie, age four, noticed for the first time the small mound of sawdust on the workbench beneath the vice where the sawing was done. She asked her teacher what it was. Debbie's teacher, Mrs. Thompson, wisely parried the question. "Mmm, yes, I see that, Debbie. That *is* interesting. What do *you* think about it?" Debbie studied the sawdust some more, puzzled. Mrs. Thompson had expressed concern, but busy with other children, simply suggested to Debbie, "See if you can figure it out." The morning period in the woodworking shop ended with nothing more said about the sawdust.

The next week the same group had their turn again. Mrs. Thompson noticed that Debbie's fascination with the sawdust had not diminished. With intent curiosity she watched as another child sawed. Mrs. Thompson's back was turned to the workbench when she heard Debbie's whoop of joyful discovery. "Mrs. Thompson, I know what it is!" With brimming satisfaction she declared, "It's the crumbs from the wood after the saw sawed it!" "You're right, Debbie. It's called sawdust."

This anecdote underlines the value of appropriate hesitancy when responding to a child's question. When we stand back, holding off with immediate answers, we give the child time to think. The week before when Debbie had first asked about the sawdust, Mrs. Thompson could have responded on the spot, "That's sawdust, Debbie." If she had, Debbie would have had an answer to her question, but think of the exploration and the observation she would have lost. Debbie would also have been denied the delight of triumph that came when she figured out the answer for herself. "It's the crumbs from the wood after the saw sawed it." When adults, eager to pass on the wealth of their experience, hover over children and are too ready with answers and suggestions, they inhibit the growth of the children's mental processes. Although it took a week Debbie not only got her answer, but also made use of a fine opportunity to exercise her deductive faculties. Children learn best through discovery.

The
Blankelee
Got Burned
Up

Chapter 3

Learning from decision making: to make the complex and numerous decisions required of them as adults, children must begin when they are very young to believe that they are capable of deciding.

JERRY's "blankelee," an old carriage robe, was his best friend in time of need. Jerry held his blankelee close to his nose and sniffed it as he sucked his thumb. After he learned to walk, the blankelee went with him up and down the stairs and flopped along the sidewalk as he trotted after the bigger kids. When it was washed Jerry was distressed, and he would let the blankelee lie until it developed the smell he liked. Eventually, his mother cut it in two and washed only half at a time. As Jerry grew, his need for the blankelee lessened. One day he announced that he did not need it any more. With determination he threw it into a corner. A day or so later, he became upset about something and went for his blankelee. The self-imposed weaning process went on for a week or so, until he felt the time had come for a final decision. Jerry, very manly and serious, walked up to his mother in the kitchen. "Mamma, I'm going to throw this blankelee out. Shall I put it in the garbage or the trash?" These were alternatives of import, for the trash was burned each day in an incinerator in the back yard, but the garbage man took away the garbage only once a week. "It's up to you, Jerry. You decide." He thought a minute, then started down the back steps with blankelee clutched in his arms. "It's going in the trash."

Jerry not only decided to throw the blankelee away and how to throw it away, but was responsible for raising the question in the first place. No one had suggested that he even consider discarding it. There are certain personal and very significant matters to a toddler that we must, if at all possible, allow him to decide for himself. Often these involve the conflict between a need of earlier babyhood and the need to grow. The story of the blankelee is one of these. Then there are other times when a youngster, because of certain circumstances precipitated by his own growth is required to make a choice. Such was the case of Sam and his bottle-diaper dilemma.

Sam was two and a-half. He had learned to stay dry during the day and wore training pants, but at night he wore diapers. Sam dearly loved his bottle of milk before sleep, so the diapers were soggy by morning. One night feeling very grown up he decided he did not want to wear the diapers. He went to bed in his training pants, but still with the bottle. The next morning the crib was sopping, the urine literally dripping onto the floor. Sam was chilled and miserable. Of course, the bottle of milk had had something to do with his misery. Sam and only Sam needed to choose between two alternatives. The next evening his mother said, "Sam, if you want the bottle at night, that's fine, but you get so wet you'll have to wear the diapers. If you would rather wear the training pants, that's fine too, but you'll have to give up the bottle." Sam contemplated these options for a while before he said he would rather wear the pants and skip the bottle. He and his mother did it that way, and he was dry and perky the next morning, happy with his new nighttime, grown-up garb. He never asked for the bottle again, and the diapers made a fine batch of cleaning rags.

These incidents reflecting the tension between growth and dependency may appear insignificant to us, but they were landmark steps for Jerry and Sam in their education for adulthood.

Ahead of them both lie many years before maturity develops, and during these years in the home as well as later in school the quality and amount of decision making allowed them will determine the extent of their personal responsibility as adults. Just as Jerry was given the freedom to decide when he was ready to throw away the blankelee and Sam made the choice between the diapers and the bottle, Randy (whose father pressured his purchase of the fire engine) should have been given the opportunity of deciding how to spend his allowance according to his own values at that time. When we allow the child early appropriate choices, we are building a firm foundation for later learning.

As children grow the choices permitted them become more complex and numerous, and the choices adults make for them decrease in number. When we send our children off to school at five or six years, we would like to assume they will be given greater and more challenging opportunities to exercise their decision-making abilities. Yet too often the public school system fails to build on children's earlier experiences and instead, for the sake of order and efficiency perhaps, limits rather than extends decision making. If we are raising children to become free men and women capable of participating intelligently in a democratic society, one may well question this lockstep approach to learning.

Education today enfolds our children within its massive structure for at least nine months of the year for twelve or thirteen years, and for the increasing number who go on to college and graduate school, a total of sixteen to twenty years. This is quite a contrast to the beginnings of public schools a hundred or so years ago, when schooling was designed to make every citizen literate by providing a few simple rudiments of the three Rs. Because the country was largely rural, most school sessions were short, squeezed into the winter months after the crops were in, and most children did not attend school beyond their early teens.

When we keep children in school as long as we do today we naturally want to be assured they are not only mastering the academic basics, but learning how to think, to judge wisely, to solve problems. When we consider the tremendous investment of time, energy and money the institution requires of our children, their families, teachers, and administrators, we are justified in concerning ourselves with the success or failure of this heavy dose of educational experience. Is it contributing in a major way to the genuine development of human beings?

The public school system is under attack from all sides. Criticism is flung from different directions, and proposals for improvement are often in diametric opposition. Where does our system for schooling our children stand? Obviously on ground less solid than we would like. Critics who have been researching the ways children learn to think and to develop creativity point to the need for more humanitarian and child-centered schools. Their contention is that teaching is not necessarily learning; that the child is being lost in a maze of rigidly controlled curricula, administered inexorably, much of it irrelevant to the child's needs. These educators suggest that the best learning is experiential and that public schools provide too little training in choosing, exploring, discovering, and evaluating.

Then there are others who fault the system for its laxity, maintaining schools are too permissive and basics are neglected. These critics equate learning with the acquisition of knowledge— learning is a product or commodity to be used, rather than an activity in which the individual participates. Widespread among them is the belief that play in early childhood is a waste of precious time.

Most recently a cry of shock has come from both sides in response to the startling fact that many of our children cannot read. And those who can, do not read very well, or very much. In spite of the acceleration of academics and heavy pressure for achievement in the schools during the several decades since Russia's Sputnik was launched, there are high school graduates who can read only on a second grade level. Although college material is being shoved down into high school and reading down into kindergarten, the scores in national achievement tests are dropping.

Right or wrong, thoughtful or superficial, the criticisms and concerns are chipping away at the same problem: how can we improve our ways of raising the young for a democratic society that values justice and the dignity of the individual? Though there is little agreement as to the causes of the problem and no singleness of purpose as to its solution, there is a kind of desperate certainty that the problem exists. If we expect to survive as a people capable of establishing and holding values consistent with a humanitarian philosophy, we must re-examine the ways in which we are educating our children. It is essential that children grow into adults who not only can read and write but who are curious and imaginative and capable of making choices based on ethical values. Here again is the recurring motif: our condemnation to freedom symbolized by the story of Adam and Eve and the fruit that gave them the knowledge of right and wrong. We must help our children learn to make wise choices between the two.

We know the early training we give children is fundamental to the development of values and to the exercise of their choosing skills. Though we may expect the schools to carry on what we have initiated at birth, we cannot depend on them to provide the bulk of education. Perhaps one of the major problems of the public education system is that our society expects too much of it. Even assuming that our schools were greatly improved, we cannot count on formal schooling to take the place of early learning. What happens to children before they are six is of awesome proportion. With the blankelees and the bottles and the decisions associated with them, parents lay the groundwork for their child's maturity of judgment.

But it is not an easy task. We, too, are products of our times. We are geared to results. Our entire society is product-oriented. If it is a tough assignment for us to stand steady on humanitarian values over the material, how much more difficult it is for the young. Children today are too often left to drift in a sea of conflicting and unsettling forces. The weakening family structure; the disappearance of a community support system; less time for inter-personal communication because of long hours of passive television viewing—all combine to leave the child uncommitted and undirected. The prevalence of these debilitating forces should prove a convincing argument to us to do all we can to strengthen the environment we provide children in their early years.

Much of this strengthening can be supplied day in and day out by the kind and number of alternatives adults provide the child. Children grow through the act rather than the end. So often when we, as adults, contemplate values we think primarily of the value itself, rather than the process of acting on a value. When we consider the matter of choices, we consider the quality of the alternatives. And when we think of creativity, we are likely to think only of the completed act. Young children do not work this way. Their world is tethered to the act, it is centered in the present. Children are strengthened by process.

Because young children do not hold values identical with those of adults or because the alternatives offered them involve such minor matters as bubble gum or jackets, it is tempting to assume that children's decision making is insignificant and not much related to their growth. We cheat the child when we persist in this short-sighted view. The soil of early childhood is fertile for beginnings of growth in intelligent choosing as we have seen in the very personal decisions Jerry and Sam were allowed to make. When these two youngsters were provided the freedom to decide, the significance of the decisions was not in the decisions per se, but in the boys' assumption of personal authority and their commitment of responsibility for their choices. The process provided the exercise. It is the decision made and followed through that bolsters children's self-esteem for they grow with the sense that they are competent to decide and to accept consequences.

MARGO is still in diapers and is trying to crawl into an adult chair. She falls back with a plop on her thick wad of protection. Without a whimper, up she gets and tries again, but cannot quite make it. "Oh," thinks Mamma, "she does so want to get up into that chair." So, swoosh, she lifts Margo up. "There you go!" Margo scowls and begins to scream. "My, didn't you *want* to sit there? Okay, down you go." Soon after that Margo tries to get into the chair again. Mother shakes her head and mutters, "I don't understand you, Baby, you want up, then you want down. You don't know what you want." Oh yes, she does. She knows exactly what she wants. I have seen other mothers do differently, aware of the choice the baby has tried to make—to get into the chair by herself. As the old saying so aptly puts it, I don't want a threaded needle, I want to thread a needle.

Given the freedom, Margo will keep trying and she will fall back, but eventually she will make it, and then as she turns around and sits high on that big chair her crows of accomplishment will light up the day. She might as well be a mountain climber reaching a peak never before reached by man. The mother will share this happy moment with her child. Then the baby will probably get down and crawl up again and again and again, until she has mastered it.

What goes into such a small episode? A child makes a choice for herself. She decides to try. She encounters a difficulty and she overcomes. She has had no sense of failure, although in fact she has failed more than once to accomplish the climb into the chair. Until an adult labels an activity failure or success, right or wrong, a child doesn't know what the words mean. When we are judgmental of children's simple activities we tend to freeze their initiative and block their resourcefulness. Children can learn to accept the consequences of failure and eliminate the anxiety of failing *if* their choices are not tagged right or wrong.

Children who choose an activity freely and cannot manage it will either try again, change course, or go on to something else. Whether practicing climbing at an early age or exploring toys when older, children need unhurried time and freedom to find their way. When an adult, meaning to be helpful, points out the right way to do something, a child automatically is put in the vulnerable position of possible failure, of doing it the wrong way. To avoid failure, the child may stop trying or lose interest in the project entirely.

Such was the case when a young acquaintance of mine came to visit with her two preschool daughters. The girls and Michael were happily bouncing around, chattering in the toy corner. The girls seemed especially interested in a small wooden train with pieces of track that fit together. Their mother, unacquainted with the toy, became fascinated. She joined the children and on her knees adeptly fastened together several pieces of the track, hooked a car to the engine, and ran the train down the track. Satisfied with herself and the toy she leaned back. "Look, girls. That's the way it goes. Isn't this a cute train?" She ran it back and forth again, "Choo, choo," and looked toward her daughters. The children had stepped back as Mother took over. Their initial curiosity about the train had vanished. They only nodded in response and were off to other things. Mother rose and shrugged, wondering at their lack of interest in the delightful train. Without meaning to, Mother had taken the initiative from the children by showing them the correct procedure for hooking the track and train together.

Peter, at age two, played simply and happily with colored blocks he had received for his birthday. He was far too young to entertain the idea of representational construction. His grandmother, in an effort to "teach" him the proper way to build identifiable structures began to build with him one day. She constructed a house with a chimney. Peter was delighted and tried to imitate the design. But he could not. Discouraged, he stopped trying and cajoled, "Gamma, you do it 'gain!" She did for several days over and over again. But eventually she became weary and bored. Peter simply was not learning at all, she realized, so she busied herself with other matters. But Peter could not go back to his simple play. Grandma's more experienced adult vision had deadened his imagination. The blocks had become something for other people to use—the tools of a spectator sport as far as he was concerned. Peter's mother stored the unused blocks away for several months until he was ready to rediscover them. When she brought them out again Peter was almost two and a-half. He had grown during that time. His perceptions and small muscles had developed and his verbal and creative abilities had expanded. He had forgotten his grandmother's patterning and was able to play with the blocks once again on his own level and without frustration. The block set provided hours of creative enjoyment for Peter. In describing the episode to me his mother added that when she brought the blocks out for the second time, she tactfully asked Grandma to leave Peter alone when he played with them. Grandma had co-operated.

In the last several decades studies concerning the development of creativity and values—both necessary for making thoughtful choices—conclude that children are by nature creative, that some are more creative than others, and that creativity can be encouraged, severely discouraged, or nearly destroyed by certain environmental conditions. Educators, parents, and researchers are becoming convinced that creativity and growth in the process of valuing are not subject, as academic skills are, to conventional tests and cannot be measured by intelligence tests or the like. Often, children who do well academically are weak in creativity. Their ability to see beyond the academic fence, to vault the immediate and use their imagination may be underdeveloped. If young children are to increase their skills in putting ideas and information together, and in seeking original and ethical solutions to problems when they are older, they will need as much freedom as possible in putting together blocks and toy trains when they are younger.

A HEARTBREAKING example of what can happen to a child when choice in certain areas is removed is the story of four-year-old Sylvia. She was a happy child and showed unusual talent with art materials. Her imagination and creativity were a constant source of pleasure to both of us. She worked with concentration and joy, blooming in the open environment of the Open Door School. The next year her mother, who had a long drive to the school, transferred her to another school. The new school was different as I found out when I visited there the next spring. The children spent half the morning on letter and number work sheets and the remaining time on patterned art. Little time was provided for dramatic play or other creative activities.

After greeting Sylvia early in the morning, I spotted her later when I wandered into the art room where the teacher was directing about fifteen children in a project. They were making pictures of aquariums by pasting a paper frame on a piece of construction paper and pasting fish inside the frame. With an expression of confusion, Sylvia was standing behind the teacher waiting her turn for directions, dangling in her hands a piece of construction paper and the cut-out frame. Finally it was her turn. "Teacher, what do I do now?" she said in a woebegone, timid voice. My heart was sad for the loss of a fine spirit of originality and independence.

A set of negative reactions exemplified by Sylvia's nervousness about the aquarium project is most often seen when an activity is dictated by an adult and completion equals success. The child may become overly dependent on the adult as Sylvia did or bored and chuck the whole thing as the little girls did with the toy train. Let children choose freely and let them fail in their way—do not let them feel they have failed in our way. Let them freely change directions or give up and go on to something else, or let them, as Margo did, persistently keep trying over and over to attain that self-appointed mountain top.

Watch the small girl with blocks setting out to build a fire truck. She places a block here, a block there, another on top, as she chatters to herself. "And now here is a wheel, one here, one . . . here, whoops, down it goes . . . then one here like this . . ." As we watch we see she is having difficulty propping up the structure as she first envisioned it. But she is flexible. "Okay, the fire engine got broke. They had to take it to the garage, it's in the garage now, so I'll make the walls for the garage, one here, one here, then another . . ." and on she goes. She had no sense of failure in our

45

sense of the word. When there are no patterns, no right way, no wrong way, an uncompleted project will not bring disaster.

While playing, the girl with the blocks very naturally utilized her ability to make decisions. She was tremendously resilient, adaptable, and imaginative when left alone. She was willing to build and design for long periods according to her inner urgings. Sylvia, on the other hand, was anxious about the aquarium. In attempting to follow an imposed pattern, she feared failure and wanted to be sure she was doing it in the right way. (In a school system that eliminated the grade *failing* and substituted *having difficulty*, the report is that the behavioral problems of those who were having difficulty were greatly decreased.)

The flexibility of small children and the ease with which they adjust to failure of their own making was obvious in an episode of play when Sean, Scott, and Danna, all age four, were trying to complete a house they had built with large, hollow blocks. Sean, a tiny child, and Scott, a husky one, were "asleep" under an old yellow bedspread in the house. Danna was continuing the construction, endeavoring to place planks across the top as a roof. Try as they might, Sean and Scott could not keep still, and the walls kept moving, unseating the planks that Danna was so carefully placing. "You two go to sleep. Be quiet, I can't get the roof to stay," Danna-Mother ordered, but without malice. "Scott, move up your feet," said Sean, wriggling in the other direction and tearing loose another side. This went on for about ten minutes. They were trying to do what they had set out to do—they wanted to do it—yet the anxiety usually present when children are attempting to follow directions was absent. Finally they gave up, calmly and matter-of-factly. The roof simply would not stay on. Danna and Scott left for the sink corner where an exciting episode of dramatic play was going on with pots, food color, and soap bubbles. Sean went off to look at a book.

If in this case a teacher had stood over the children, directing the course of the play, advising on means of solving the problem, encouraging continuation of the project after the children had decided to stop, they would have met failure. They would have lost their sense of competence. Instead, they were left in their play to find their way and to deal with the consequences.

The bubble gum does count. And so do the blocks, the blankelees, and the bottles. They count very much, not because of their intrinsic value, but because they are objects for decisions we allow our young children. Parents must stand back for a few minutes in each case and ask themselves, "Is this a decision my child should make for himself, or herself?" If the conclusion is yes, then allow the child freedom to follow through. When we do this we are helping children build capability, confidence, and a sense of responsibility they are going to need in good measure all through life.

ONE of the first matters confronting a child who enters school concerns the readiness to learn certain academic subjects, especially reading. If Randy's initiatives are to count or Danna's or Sam's, their sense of the right time for them to learn to read should be respected, for they are the only ones who know when they are ready. If children are fortunate enough to be in a classroom with an understanding and skilled teacher, there will be many alternatives for learning activities. When as a result of those experiences added to those they have been exposed to at home, something comes together inside, something clicks in their minds, they will know they are ready to read, and the teacher will be there to assist. I have observed over many years that children whose development is proceeding in a normal, healthy way, who are read to at home, and who are free to decide when they were ready, always learn to read.

Our society has made a fetish of the ability to read at a given age. To read at six has become the hallmark of intelligence, of success for children and parents. If a child is not ready to read and does not learn to do so at this precise time, anxiety like a fog envelops the child and all those around him or her. Parents are tense, teachers are afraid, the school's reputation is questioned.

The build-up for the critical test at six begins in nursery school where many parents reveal their nervousness. "Will our Mary learn to read? When? Are you preparing her to learn to read? Is she playing too much? What can we do to help her read earlier?" To read in the first grade is anticipated as proof of achievement and it may overshadow concerns for other aspects of development.

Teachers and parents are usually delighted and somewhat awed when a four or five year old learns to read on his or her own. It is a happy surprise. Why is this? I suspect it is because we have been conditioned to believe that learning to read is a long, diffi- cult, pit-ridden road of anguish for a child to go down at a pre- scribed time. Consequently, when a child in nursery school mi- raculously starts reading, our response is one of wonder. That reaction mirrors the common (but mistaken) belief that children do not learn anything unless we teach them. Children who teach themselves to read are interested and ready. Their experiences and observations have led them right into visual comprehension of the symbols of their native language. There is no miracle in- volved. I am convinced that many more children would read spontaneously, if we would only give them the time. When we push children to learn at six, and they are not ready and do not learn, our pushing grinds them down to failure. The failure is a severe blow to their self-esteem which further serves to make it more difficult than ever for them to learn to read. The label, *failure*, can atrophy the mind of a young child.

It is my hunch that there are two main reasons why many children today are not reading well or not reading much. The first is their sense of defeat when they do not learn on schedule. The second is the many, many hours of television they are watching. It is not so much the content of the programs that retards readiness to read, but the simple fact that when children are passively watching television they are not doing all the other things that build toward reading—playing, talking, discovering, relating to others, and being read to.

How silly it would be if we tried to teach children to talk which is, after all, one of the first steps toward reading. Just suppose the kit manufacturers who prey on parents' fears and ambitions were to devise "sound yet simple" lesson plans for parents to teach their children to talk, EARLY. I can see the blurbs: "Just ten minutes a day, right after his morning feeding, beginning with Do, do, do, going into Mi, mi, mi, and through the other consonants—to be reviewed each Saturday morning. It's easy, Mother, give your child the head start he deserves."

But we parents do not do that because we respect our babies too much. A baby, let us say a girl, is allowed to decide when she is hungry, then we feed her. When she is sleepy, we give her a place to take a nap. When her coos turn into babbles and we distinguish various consonants and vowels deliberately and thoughtfully put together, we know that she will soon be talking, and we respond with our own words. Of course we have been talking to her since birth, for that is how she had been learning. She has understood our words for some time, and now she is teaching herself to talk. We help her naturally by our attitude, our response to her verbalizations, and by giving her freedom to explore, touch, smell, see, and taste, for talking cannot be isolated from her development and her interaction with her environment any more than reading can be.

The role of parents and teachers is nurturing rather than didactic. We provide the framework of materials, the atmosphere of love and acceptance, arranging the scene and setting the stage for discovery and growth. We are the facilitators, the listeners, the responders. But the motivation, the choice comes from the children who must believe they are capable. Otherwise there will be no real learning.

I'd
Rather
Do It
Myself

Chapter 4

Learning from playing: to enliven and integrate real and imaginary experiences, children participate in the process of play.

Play is the very stuff of childhood. Time for playing and freedom during this time is crucial to the healthy growth of children. When we attempt to direct children's play we are violating rights that are unquestionably theirs. It is through the dynamics of play—the ebb and flow, the give and take, and the opportunities it provides for flexibility, for imaginative change in direction —that children integrate their experiences. Through play children expand their minds, develop verbal abilities, learn to know themselves and begin to learn to handle and work out relationships with others. Though well-meaning, the adult who interferes and suggests, "Why don't you do it *this* way?" or, "Put that piece up here," or "Can't you figure *that* out?" is committing a kind of castration of childhood.

We all know that a child who does not play is in trouble. Yet, even with this knowledge, adults too often intrude into the world of the playing child with advice and ideas, robbing the child of freedom to grow and learn through this natural medium. It has been pointed out that playfulness in the young of different species is in direct proportion to the intelligence of the species. Kittens and puppies, for example, spend relatively more time playing than do guinea pigs and chickens who seem not to play at all. Human children require long periods of playing over many years before they fully mature.

I would like to share with you an excerpt from an article I wrote, titled "Some Observations Upon the Value of Children's Play," published in the February 1973 issue of *Young Children:*

> The many facets of children's play are intriguing and varied—from the absorbed explorations of the toddler as he examines a piece of dust, holding it with great precision between his thumb and index finger, then dropping it, again carefully retrieving it; the excitement of the group of fours as they build with hollow blocks, working together, carried forward with the enthusiasm of their ideas; the small girl sitting alone, rocking her doll to sleep.
>
> What really *is* play? No one, I am sure, knows precisely. It cannot be dissected, catalogued, and wrapped up in a neat package for marketing. It is too complex, too subjective, too variable an experience to lend itself to cool, precise definition. Its values to a child in any particular situation can be sensed, sometimes more intuitively than intellectually. Often, though, what happens to a child during a particular episode of play may not be fully understood until months or even years later.
>
> To ask the question, what is play, is somehow like asking what is life? For play to a child is an intrinsic part of his life as he weaves his way through time and space. An episode of play may involve specific learning, again,

it may involve the development of attitudes, but always it is experiential.

Often work has some of the attributes of play; but in work there is usually a premeditated product sought, or goal involved—a clean floor, a car off the assembly line, memorization for a good grade on a test. But play is not an end of an activity or the result of an experience; it is the activity and the experience itself and involves the whole-hearted participation of the individual in the process. It is movement—physical, emotional, mental, or a combination of these. It is movement of a child alone, or with other children, alone or in harmony with his environment, or against it. It is basically self-initiated with a high quotient of spontaneity and improvisation. Because there is no imposed blueprint, there is no right, no wrong, no fear of failure that results from trying to follow a pattern. There is freedom for decision making.

THE commercial toy, boxed and sold complete with illustrated directions is a good example of unnecessary interference in children's play. Although such directions meddle less in a child's world than an adult who gets down on the floor with a child and calls the shots, printed instructions discourage originality and problem solving and in some children create unbearable frustration. I have seen children cry with rage because of their failure to duplicate the pictures in a guide book. And when the attack of defeat and desperation is over they rarely want to play with the toy again. It is a good idea to remove and destroy the directions that come with the purchase before children see them.

Mud, water, pots and pans, boxes, and transparent tape are toys on the home front that happily have escaped the authority of the toy designers. Perhaps that is the reason mothers say when talking of their young, "Bobby plays so happily with just boxes, it's amazing!" No one thinks of writing directions for play with sand or cooking vessels.

A relative sent Tommy a small erector set. He had opened the box before his mother had a chance to remove the directions, and Tommy latched onto the brightly illustrated little booklet. (In all fairness a parent cannot take the directions away once the child has seen them.) Tommy was intrigued by the intricate construction models. After carefully unpacking all the pieces and arranging them neatly in the center of the dining room floor, he set to work enthusiastically with the booklet open before him. His mother watched apprehensively from the kitchen.

His endeavor was doomed. At his age he could not possibly imitate the sophisticated pictured constructions. He worked patiently at first, but tears and screams of frustration came when he realized that no matter how hard he tried his product did not mirror the pattern. His travails as he stubbornly continued were heart-rending, but because of his particularly determined nature his mother was unable to distract him from his aim or even help him out. Rigid with trying and exasperated with failing, he finally threw the whole project in the corner and himself on the floor, howling.

The next day no one seemed to know where the erector set was, and Tommy did not really care. Months passed before his mother brought it out of hiding, minus directions. Without them, Tommy felt free to follow his own inclinations and spent hours in simple and primitive construction. Though his products would probably have horrified the author of the pattern booklet, his wobbly, little vehicles were beautiful to him. He then gained a sense of achievement.

ANY school, such as a Montessori, that requires children to use a certain piece of learning equipment only in a certain way provides another example of how we take choices away from children; it becomes the adult's decision that the child shall learn a particular thing from a particular toy in a particular way. The geometrical sorting board in my classroom has been used for its designated purpose only occasionally. Instead its pieces have become many things, such as sandwiches on an imaginary boat ride, rattles for babies, and pieces of an elaborate mosaic of colored blocks. Those imaginative uses are at least of equal importance to the use of the board as a tool for teaching geometric shapes. It will require a variety of experiences, games, and observations for a child to organize his concept of geometric form. The sorting board is only one in a cumulative process.

Children do not learn in an orderly sequence, or at least in the kind of orderly sequence recognizable to most adults. To us, their learning may appear random, yet it is guided by the internally initiated explorations unique to each child that adults can only infrequently glimpse. When a child is ready, and has absorbed a variety of experiences relating to a certain concept, he or she will bring the separate learnings together—maybe sooner, maybe later—and a particular concept will become intrinsic to the child's growing self.

One windy March morning it was tellingly revealed to me what a delightful experience for a child the integrative process can be at the moment of discovery. I had taken a group of three-year-olds for a walk. We had gone up the street on the sidewalk about a block from the school to the firehouse. Because the firemen were busy doing their weekly cleaning that day, we did not go in, but walked to the rear of the building, examined their hoses hanging out to dry, marvelled at the size of the mops they used to scrub the floor, then returned to the school the back way, through a wooded area.

When we once again stood at the door to the school, Lindy paused, a contemplative expression on her face. She looked back through the trees to the fire station from where we had come, then in the other direction, the route taken when we left. Her face lit up, and with exuberance she cried out, "We made a whole circle! All of us made a real, whole circle!"

I am sure that Lindy's experiences with the geometric sorting board had contributed to this vivid revelation of what a circle is, made by people walking. But it could not have done the whole job. Lindy had been storing up many experiences with circles, all contributing to her flash of understanding.

CHILDREN need unhurried periods to explore and experiment with objects, toys, or materials, to "mess around" as David Hawkins so aptly puts it in his article, "Messing Around In Science."

I'd Rather Do It Myself

Messing around may seem aimless to adults, yet from the perspective of children, it is not so at all. After handling and examining an object, a new toy, or mechanism, a child may wander off, later to return to handle and examine it some more. A total concept is not learned by a single discovery, but by many smaller ones. In this connection Hawkins believes "all of us must cross the line between ignorance and insight many times before we truly understand."

To provide the kind of materials and freedom that encourage children to putter and explore, giving them time to cross that line "between ignorance and insight" on their own, is a far better approach to raising children than the purchase of "scientifically designed education kits." These kits, around which early childhood and elementary curricula in schools are too frequently designed are also advertised for home use. The quite erroneous presumption is that the designers of these kits have an inside track on the sequence of a child's learning. (And it costs parents mightily for the privilege of sharing this inside track.) The use of inexpensive and available materials—sand, water, scrap wood, sawdust, dough and clay, boxes, and pieces of fabric, plus some basic commercial equipment such as blocks, vehicles and dolls—is less costly and allows children freedom to develop a learning sequence in accord with their individual inner patterns rather than the imposed patterns of the kit designer.

Much of what boys and girls learn in their play and in their messing around goes unseen. The teacher may have no idea that a child has picked up and manipulated certain objects, explored and mused on certain ideas. Perhaps something the mother reports from home or some fleeting glimpse the teacher gets from something the child does or says will tell her something is happening. Because we sometimes see it happen, I have faith in its happening constantly.

Four-year-old Scott made it clear to me one day that over a period of months he had been putting together small discoveries concerning the properties of air. His mother was driving several of our class to the turkey farm. Scott was in the front seat. It was a warm day. Mother had turned on the air conditioner, and Scott was fiddling with it. "No, Scott," his mother said, "leave that alone." Scott paid no attention and continued to fiddle, feeling the flowing air on his hand and face. After some thought he said, "Mamma, did you know that air is invisible?" "Oh, is it?" "Yes, it's all around, but we can't see it."

It was then as I listened from the back seat that I became aware of the connections Scott was making between the air conditioner and experiences he had earlier in the school year: a trip to a small airport; puttering around with balloons, blowing them up, feeling the air he could not see gush out; winding up the propellers of small balsa planes, watching them spin through the invisible substance that surrounds us; playing with tire pumps; blowing his breath on his hands and bubbles in water. Scott had been tying his experiences together, and he shared them with his mother when he told her, "Mamma, did you know that air is invisible?"

In the exploration of a physical phenomenon a child will frequently answer his or her own question with a misconception, such as, "Hey, which is heavier? *This* is heavier, because it's bigger." The wise adult, rather than correcting this thinking, will devise experiments involving weight and bulk, so that the child, let us say a boy named Jack, may discover those relationships on his own. A kitchen scale, rocks of various sizes, pieces of wood, and a large styrofoam block will be sufficient.

Another reason for not jumping in immediately and correcting Jack's conclusion is that by so doing we are inadvertently criticizing his ability to reason. When you stop and think, based on his experience it is logical that the bigger will also be the heavier. Pointing out his ignorance pains him. What we must try to do is give him more experience by providing the materials for experimentation so that he may, on his own, rectify his misconception.

THERE is a certain sense of discovery and wonder when a child glimpses his or her own growth by recalling what he or she "used to think," or "used to play." For instance, there is the four-year-old girl who remembered that when she was two she used to think the mail was sent from place to place in pipes, just as the water came to the houses. This sort of looking back revealed an awareness of self and growth that could only result from her drawing together, reappraising, and re-evaluating the dynamic threads of her experience.

During preparation for dinner one night, ten-year-old Michael revealed his insights into what he used to play at four. Michael had been in bed for a week with the flu. His first afternoon up, he was raring to go, cheerful, talkative, and delighted to be downstairs into what seemed a whole new world. He could not go outside, but was happy flopping around in his bathrobe and slippers. As supper got underway he suggested we eat in the dining room and that he set the table "in a fancy manner."

"Go to it," I said, and he did. He got out the best silver, best dishes, and arranged a centerpiece of tarnished silver tea pot, Indian corn, and artificial daffodils. As his enthusiasm mounted, ideas came pouring out. "Let's call this a restaurant. We'll have printed menus and all that, and when Daddy and Pete come home, we'll pretend we're going out to eat, and I'll be the high class waiter."

A whole complicated fabric of a game was built upon the original offer to set the table fancy. Michael was completely absorbed. Signs appeared advertising Maison de Rileyeuse. Daddy and Pete, home from work, allowed themselves to be ushered into the living room via the back pantry way and were served sherry with an olive. Then seated at a candlelit table in Maison de Rileyeuse, we were served as promised in truly high class fashion by our high class waiter with a large red napkin over his forearm and still wearing his blue terrycloth bathrobe and slippers.

That was the sometimes play of a ten-year-old boy who was usually happiest with a group of other boys, falling and yelling outside. As I observed the development of his ideas as he constructed the details of the restaurant game, the highlight of the evening to me (aside from the sheer fun of the project which we all enjoyed) was Michael's moment of insight that came somewhere in the midst of preparation. He stopped what he was doing, looked thoughtful for a moment, and said, "Isn't it funny, Mother, a couple of years ago I was all excited about playing cowboys and all that, and now I'm playing restaurant. And it's for *real*."

From where he stood when he was four, the cowboy games were real. The restaurant game was real to him at ten. It is this essence of realness that exists at the height of spontaneous dramatic play—the forward movement of creative ideas centered in improvisation—that makes for the precious spirit of genuine play. At nineteen Michael is able to look back upon Maison de Rileyeuse with the same kind of chuckle and wonder that he felt for his cowboy games when he had outgrown them. As play thrives on immediacy, insight in later years into the validity of past experi-

ence is heightened by a sensitive awareness of changing realities—
the "used to play" and the "used to think."

THOUGH I am urging parents and teachers to keep hands off
when children play so they may have the freedom to make decisions, to improvise, and to think and act upon their own initiative, I do not mean that we are uninvolved. Before play begins, we
are especially involved. We parents and teachers set the stage by
providing equipment and materials, after having given time and
thought to their selection. We set the boundaries for play by establishing some firm, necessary rules. We structure the *environment*, but we do not structure the *process of the play itself*. Once
the play has begun, we shift our involvement to a peripheral position. We are available when needed, sometimes to redirect and
for safety reason to say Stop! Children's play, as we all know,
can sometimes become chaos. We must be aware of what is going
on and be ready to jump in and help out. But only if necessary.
Using this kind of sensitivity, we will be sufficiently involved.

As with love, play can be a many-splendored thing with
many faces and ages. Play must be alive and come from inside,
and, as love, it can never be a spectator sport. It is active and self-
initiated. Watching a football game may be fun, but it is not play.
We cannot program play, just as we cannot program love. We
cannot impose upon children what we think they need to play, or
what we think they should feel about play.

Play is the doing. "I'd rather do it myself, Mother," is packed
with meaning. We cannot hand the child an idea or a word and

expect it automatically to become a part of the child. Children may accept our offering, but they are the only ones capable of the incorporation of the idea into their growing selves. For the young child, play is the single most effective means to accomplish integration and growth.

Fences
Without
Fights

Chapter 5

**Leadership or Permissiveness: to understand and affirm
a true idea of freedom, children must have the security
of loving, thoughtful, and appropriate prohibitions.**

O NE summer I met a young couple with a daughter who was
three years old. This couple was intent upon raising their
child in the "permissive" method, so popular in the '40s and '50s.
She was allowed to determine all her routines, even when it was
embarrassingly obvious, at the expense of her mother and father.
They were most patient and understanding and very much at the
child's beck and call. One night the couple were with guests in
the living room after a fine dinner. Everyone present was an adult
except for the child. It was late for one so young, but she insisted
she was not ready for bed. She sat by her mother, asking for this
and that, joining in the conversation. Periodically, fatigue would
overcome her; her eyelids would droop and she would fall off to
sleep. A loud laugh would startle her and up she would pop. This
happened several times, each time her Mother asked, "Don't you
want to go up now, dear?"

"No, not ready," was her determined response.

Soon again she would droop. Finally her father said he would
lie down with her for a while upstairs. That suited her perfectly,
and they left. Down they both came twenty minutes later, the
child still not "ready."

This is tyranny by a child, unknowingly encouraged by conscientious parents confused by the idea of freedom. Some options may be damaging to a young child and are certainly difficult for the parent. Babies in the first months of life know when they need to eat and sleep—they are not yet interested in participating in the adult world. But when a child reaches the age of two or three and is reluctant to leave the social world for sleep, bedtime becomes a matter for the parents to establish. The episode reveals a misplacement of freedom and distorts the meaning of *permissive*. Freedom of choice in certain prescribed areas does not mean unbridled domination of the child over the parents or over the routines of family life.

Young children need the security of having certain decisions made for them, of knowing the limits beyond which they may not go. Just as children require the security of being loved and cared for, so do they require solid boundaries. These needs are best met by adults with a firm hand, without nagging moralism and whining lectures. A positive, matter-of-fact no is a blessing the child will thrive on.

It is often just as difficult for those of us who deal with children to assume authority, as it is to allow them open areas for decision making. We are in the bewildering position of making up our minds as to whether it is *our* decision or *theirs*.

While we must generally leave children alone to do their own choosing in matters of play, working with art materials, toys, dress, how much they eat, and so on, we need to take a positive hold on the portions of a child's life for which we are responsible. For parents of the very young this is a vast expanse that shrinks as the child grows and takes more responsibility. By the time the child reaches adulthood, the need for parental decision making will have completely evaporated.

When we are sure of our ground and certain the decision is ours, then simple noes and yesses reflect our convictions, rather than an open-ended, "No, don't you dare do that. I've told you a thousand times" or "No, I am not going to buy any candy today. You're always begging, 'gimme this' and 'gimme that,' what do you think I'm made of, money?" and so on.

Unequivocal noes need not be accusatory of the child's motives. They can be given simply, unadorned with emotion. It is possible to establish firm limits that respect the dignity of the little person, stated without the kind of character assasination that so hurts the boy's or girl's self-image. The child who innocently asks to be driven to the park does not need to be bombarded with, "I will *not* drive you to the park; it's too hot, and I'm tired. Why can't you leave me alone? You're a very selfish girl, always asking me to do this and do that. If you weren't so lazy, you'd walk," and on and on. A simple "No, I can't drive you to the park today, but you may walk if you like" would be so much kinder and more effective. Recriminatory noes create guilt that has no part in the raising of a healthy child.

Areas of parental determination are not only those that fall naturally within the adult domain because of their magnitude, but also family routines, such as bedtimes and mealtimes, involving the convenience of other members of the family, as well as matters of safety. A child's freedom in relation to siblings and parents must go no further than the protection of the rights of others will allow. We have all seen the poverty of children who have had their own way too much and developed no sense of fair play or respect for others. Such children's abilities to manipulate other people for their own ends may appear harmless and sometimes even cute at the age of three, but can develop into insufferable and impossible domination of their families and peers by the age of fifteen.

As necessary and desirable as they are, prohibitions must be given without threats. When children are threatened they are challenged, and a challenge is a choice. When children do not have a choice they should not be led to assume there is one.

The toddler who is about to turn the knob on the gas stove hears her mother from across the kitchen. "No, Janie! Don't you dare turn that on, or I'll spank!" The mother makes no move toward the child, but her frown, her tone, and her threat are a challenge. Janie pauses, somewhat defensively, and you can almost see her thinking: "Shall I mind her, or shan't I? Mamma's all the way across the room; it's the fun of turning on the gas or the bad of getting the spanking. Do I have any gumption, or am I a pushover?" If she does have gumption, as most small children do, she will probably turn the knob.

Had the mother, rather than challenging Janie from a distance, moved to the stove and unemotionally removed the child from the area and then stated firmly, "Stoves are not for playing; they're for cooking," the child would have had no opportunity to choose between obeying or disobeying. There would have been no need for defiance, and Janie probably would have learned something more about stoves.

A threat almost always presents a choice. "Don't you dare cross the railroad tracks, or I'll clobber you when you get back!" What is the choice, to cross the tracks and get clobbered or not to cross the tracks? Sometimes too, a threat not only serves to give a choice, but can become a suggestion. Perhaps it had not occurred to the child to cross the tracks, but, "Mmm," the child thinks, "that's not such a bad idea, come to think of it." A firm no should not provide either choices or suggestions.

Also, there are times when parents muddy the waters of control by their own insecurity. The apparent weakness of their egos and the need for bolstering interferes with their setting stable, impersonal boundaries. In such instances the parents' primary concern seems to be obedience as such, rather than the enforcement of rules. These parents appear to be convinced that "Janie's got to do that because *I said so!* She's got to learn to mind!" When that is the case, boundaries then become battlefields for a contest of wills between parents and children. If the children obey, the parents have won a round in their quest for status, but the children are left feeling they have been railroaded, bullied, and that they are weaklings. Children should be able to obey without having to feel that way.

Emotionally charged contention between parents and children brings problems with it. At one extreme such conflict may crush the children, breaking their spirit and sense of independence and initiative. At the opposite extreme the constant battling for ascendancy will encourage defiance and negativism in children that in later years will spill over into relationships outside the family. It is quite possible to provide boundaries—discipline if you wish to call it that—that will preserve both the children's and the parents' self-esteem and peace in the family.

I watched a two-year-old boy in a store several months ago. While his mother paid for her purchases at the check-out counter, the child was gently pushing the top flap of a cardboard box nearby. The flap went back and forth, flip-flop. From the counter the mother demanded sharply, "Don't touch! I told you not to touch!" The child looked toward his mother, a bit surprised, then stiffened at her tone. Looking her straight in the eye he said, "No," but he made no move to touch the flap again. Although his verbal response was negative, he had obeyed his mother. "Don't you talk back to me," the mother snapped. "No, no, no," the child repeated, defiance in his assertion. Infuriated, the mother lunged toward the child and yanked him away from the box. As she pulled him from the store crying, I heard her nagging lecture above the child's screams, "You've got to learn not to talk back to me. I won't have it, no I won't. Got to learn . . ."

71

If the mother had been concerned primarily with the question of damage the child might have done the box—it was difficult for me, however, to see any objection to his exploration of the flopping top—she could simply have taken his hand, moved him away from the box, and said, "We don't play with boxes in stores." Or, when he stopped flip-flopping the box top she could have dropped the matter. Her real concern, or so it appeared, was not the enforcement of rules, but her position as boss. Her child was to obey immediately, quietly, and without demur. As the two left the store the arena for warfare between mother and child was staked out for action for the rest of the shopping trip.

Parents who feel secure in their authority, since they are after all older, wiser, and more experienced, do not need to fight for control. Bullying is unnecessary. A young child wants to feel sure the parent is in charge with a confident hand. A child simply does not need the kind of choices implicit in a threat. He does not really want the responsibility of deciding between obedience or defiance.

It sometimes demands Solomon's wisdom to determine where the rightful areas of parental decision are because there is so much variation in children's personalities, in age groups, and in situations. Once determined, however, it is a mark of assurance to maintain a straightforward, unwavering attitude. Rules and prohibitions for children should not be clothed in tones of self-righteousness and justified with moralistic argument. It is much better to say to the teenager, "I know you want to go out, but our rule is no going out on school nights," rather than, "I have no truck with those kids who wander all over town and stay out till all hours. They always end up in trouble, and I'm not going to have it. You're staying in, so don't you dare say another word."

Arguing, or allowing oneself to be drawn into an argument after saying no or after making a firm request is another way of letting the child know you are not quite sure of yourself and that you are leaving the door open to challenge. Take that old buga-boo, the garbage, put off too long by the child. Mother says, "Joe, that garbage must go out right now. It's overflowing." This can be said simply as fact with no comment as to how long Joe has procrastinated, how lazy he is or, "Why do I have to speak to you a thousand times?" It must be put as a parent's decision. Now, Joe will pick up the garbage in a slow, gangling way as ten-year-olds are wont to do, realizing this is it. But he will still argue as he wan-ders toward the door in circles, garbage in hand, "Why do I always have to take out the garbage? It's a rotten job, why can't Sally take out the garbage? Why always me? I have a lot of homework . . ." If he's a good talker he can squeeze in a lot of rhetoric before he gets to the garbage can. The sensible parent will refrain from re-sponding, confident that it is unnecessary to explain the request. It does not need justification.

On the other hand, if Joe's mother cannot resist picking up the gauntlet Joe has thrown down and says, "Now, stop complain-ing. Sally has her own job; we all have to cooperate in this house. Your father and I have more responsibility than . . ." she is open-ing the question for debate and defending her position just as Joe is pleading his. Argument allows for choices where there should not be any. Let Joe have the last word. He needs it. Mother does not.

It has been my observation that children who feel their opin-ions and choices are respected in the personal areas discussed in the first chapters of this book are children who are best able to cooperate more or less agreeably with family rules when they are fair and simply stated. Although children, in a very natural effort to define their independence, may sometimes argue and assert themselves loudly, they are on the whole reasonable. We parents will eliminate the challenge that invites contention by defining boundaries with kindness and without harsh character judgment. When we understand and affirm the individuality of children and evince concern for their dignity in applying prohibitions, the chances are good that their response to us will be in kind.

It All
Takes
Time

Chapter 6

Time, television, temper, and perversity:
to develop social skills, children must have
time to be with other children.

YOUNG children need a generous portion of unhurried time to
spend with one another. They need freedom to interact socially and as much opportunity as possible (appropriate to their
ages) to work on solving the inevitable problems that such interaction brings. The very young ones need experiences in learning
to share, in taking turns, and in tasting the first joys of fellowship.
If they are to grow in the ability to sustain satisfying interpersonal
relationships as they grow in years, they need time to develop
creative and imaginative ways of coping with the tensions that
prolonged periods of social living bring.

Social skills are not wrought miraculously overnight, and
there is no particular age when full social maturity is achieved.
Growth of the abilities to interact, to communicate, to share, and
to experience concern for others is an assignment we all work on
throughout our lives. The child must begin early. A baby takes
the first tentative steps into the world of others when he or she
reaches beyond the parental bond into the world of siblings and
others in the family or neighborhood circle. Later at around two
years, the child ventures into the society of peers with side-by-side
play, where company is kept but each plays independently and
alone. Social interaction is limited to disputes over toys, screams

of frustration, and cries of "Mine!" This egocentric configuration, though often exasperating to the adult, does satisfy the social bent of the toddler. It gives way slowly at three to snatches of cooperative play, more verbal communication, and genuine sustained delight in the company of peers. Still further down the road, the four- or five-year-old blossoms into the sophisticated, imaginative, cooperative group player. The child who has not had sufficient time to grow through these stages of interaction has been denied the satisfaction of a very basic human need.

Many opportunities for young children to interact with one another are provided quite naturally. Toddlers are exposed to the play of their older siblings and participate in their primitive way or simply observe from their high chairs. Later they may test their social skills when visiting relatives or friends. They may spend time in the back yard with neighbor children and eventually attend a nursery school. Parents are often concerned when they live in a neighborhood where there are no other children to provide social opportunities; hence a nursery experience several mornings a week becomes especially important. Many of us have witnessed the social deprivation of a child raised in an isolated area without contact with other children, who when enrolled in school, is excessively shy and fearful. Instinctively, most parents seem to sense the social needs of their children and seek experiences that will satisfy these needs.

Yet today, in spite of this understanding, we systematically deny opportunities for relating socially by granting children unlimited access to television. The extensive use of television for the entertainment of young children is disturbing and frightening. The content of many television programs has been severely criticized; however, to me it is not the content that should be the primary object of concern, but rather the simple fact that too many children are watching too much. Television steals irretrievable hours of life that children would spend playing, interacting emotionally and intellectually, responding to their environment, talking, laughing, facing social dilemmas, and trying out a variety of ways to solve them. Statistics have it that by age five a boy or girl has watched television for as many hours as it will take to earn a Bachelor's degree. This sizeable investment of time, lost to the flickering, one-dimensional world of the screen, should be reserved for developing children's potential as thinking, problem-solving, social beings.

I do not disagree with those who criticize the content of television by pointing out its violence, the simplistic solutions to complex human problems, the sexism and materialism of commercials. These objections are valid, but even if the content were improved drastically, I would continue my opposition to large doses of television for young children. The harm to the child is in the waste of time needed for growing. The increase in juvenile crime during the last several decades and the abusive aggression of more and more students in the schools has in part been blamed by some on the violent content of television. That may be one aspect of a complex phenomena; another may be that it is less the nature of the programs than it is the hours spent before the tube, thus denying them the time necessary to become socially civilized. They have been too busy watching television to participate in the dramas of reality. Even when several children are watching the same program together, they are relatively isolated from one another in their passive absorption.

Whether we are for or against it, television is here to stay. Because of this element of permanency we must guard against its becoming a controlling force in our lives. Above all, we must not allow it to eat into those first, precious years of our children's lives.

Children before five years of age, when they are the most vulnerable, are just beginning to sort out the real from the unreal. Television does not help in this search, but rather intensifies confusion that the children are not even conscious of. Rooted before the screen, quiet and immobile, they are passive spectators of an unreal world that passes for real because their perceptions and experience are immature.

Even the so-called educational programs, though harmless in content, are poor substitutes for time that could be spent actively occupied in the real world. Those programs honestly seek to teach, yet their dizzying, frenetic flashes of alphabet animals and numbers popping on the screen become pacifiers. It would be a better learning experience for a boy or girl to take a walk in the garden and count the first five daffodils growing in the spring and sniff their scent than to sit and watch the jazzy parade of 5s on the tube.

Television of course can be a tremendous help to parents of young children. A day with one or more preschoolers is demanding and exhausting. The relief of an hour from shouts, tears, constant chatter, and frequent squabbles can be a blessing to a tired mother, especially on a rainy day. A few moments of peace may work toward a more constructive and loving atmosphere. But will television become a Pied Piper we wish we had never invited into our homes? Do the advantages compensate for the risks? I have known families who have said no to television, and after the first shock of withdrawal, found family life greatly improved. These parents tell us their children are playing more creatively, reading more, and there is less noise and tension in the house. Teachers of these children in nursery school report that the children are playing more peacefully and imaginatively and exhibiting more independence.

In this book my argument has been toward offering young children more decision-making opportunities in personal areas than we usually do. Let Randy decide for himself how to spend his allowance and give Emily the freedom to wear the shocking pink pants with the purple shirt if that is her desire. But whether they watch television or not, and how much, is a decision for the adults in the family. If we are convinced that less television, or no television, is the best choice for Randy and Emily, then we need to make that clear and firm, without vacillation.

When children play together they are constantly making choices: to accept another child's suggestion, to resist with a counter suggestion, to hit back if given a push or not to hit back, to grab or not to grab a toy, to cooperate or to lead in an episode of play, to withdraw when frustrated or to cry in protest. The dynamics of a child's progression during social intercourse are not simple, and his or her choices throughout are based on temperament and age, social experience, and mood. Children are not born with skills in social relating. The development and refinement of social skills take a lot of time and a lot of growing. Children not only need opportunities to play but a good measure of freedom during that time to take responsibility for the choices they make while interacting with their peers.

Freedom, however, is not a license for the child to rule the roost. A complete hands-off policy would be counter-productive, especially for young children. Some scuffling and hitting between two children can often settle a dispute. But when it seems to be getting out of hand, parents and teachers must be ready to separate the warring parties. We adults walk a delicate line when we supervise children's play. We must intervene at a certain point when children are fighting, yet when they are constructing a house with blocks and their enthusiasm and ideas run ahead of their abilities to balance the structure, it is best for us to stifle our inclination to suggest a solution. Help in this case would be interference.

When a child, a girl for example, is having an especially bad day, and when with all her best efforts and ours she cannot quite make it with other children, she needs to be removed from the play group. Removed, *not* reoccupied before the television. Although she may protest, she is very likely grateful for adult restraint. She welcomes the knowledge that there is someone nearby who will help subordinate her potentially violent impulses. After she has been removed, has quieted down, and is in some measure in control of her feelings, the decision to return to the group should be hers. We ought not to decide for her that she must stay out of the action two minutes, or ten, or all morning. We should just say, "Let me know when you feel ready to return."

When we are not quite sure whether quarrelling children need our help, it is quite all right to express hesitancy, or to be *puzzled* as James L. Hymes, Jr., the early childhood expert, recommends frequently in his writings. Be tentative. Do not dive in unless you are sure you really need to. Just walking toward children in a relaxed, concerned way will often help the children settle the problem themselves. The presence of an adult may offer the support children need to work out their difficulties. A word or two, never accusatory, for we are rarely sure what provoked the fracas in the first place, most often quiets rufflled feelings and flying fists. Disputing youngsters are quite responsive to, "It seems to me you two have a problem. What's it all about?" The adult in this case is not criticizing or taking sides, but simply recognizing the children's troubles and their feelings. Often this one question will start the youngsters talking about their argument, and they will be able to settle it verbally, without hitting and without the adult's active participation.

Frequently when children run into trouble, the adult on hand is more of a catalyst and less of an arbitrator. Such was the situation the morning Frank upset Sonjia. He was five years old and an unusually bright and perceptive child with a delightful sense of humor. At certain times, though, he had difficulty controlling his temper. He was a big child and his furies could be frightening to other children. While on the kindergarten playground that morning, Frank, for no apparent reason, grabbed Sonjia's doll and gleefully threw it over the fence. Sonjia, a placid child who rarely provoked aggression from anyone, wept. It was her new doll.

Frank seemed immediately sorry and even surprised by his action. I told Sonjia I was sorry it had happened; then took Frank's hand and we walked out of the playground. I had not said a word to him. Somehow I felt he needed the opportunity to handle this himself, though there was no question in my mind that he must retrieve the doll. Once outside the gate he ran ahead and announced, "I'll get the doll." As we walked back he asked, "Will you make me sit on the bench when we get back?" The bench was the outdoor cooling off or "thinking spot." "I'm not sure, Frank." I exhibited puzzlement. He said, "I think I should think for awhile." "Suppose you give Sonjia the doll, and I'll meet you at the bench." Sonjia thanked him, and he was pleased with that. Then we met at the bench. We sat. After several minutes he said, "I think I've had my think." Frank was happy and busy the rest of the morning.

In this situation, the adult authority was there if needed, but Frank had made the important decisions: to get the doll, to sit and think, and to terminate his thinking. Frank could not have handled this responsibility at the beginning of the year, but by spring he was ready. Frank was learning more about himself, and also something about justice.

WHEN trouble erupts between children and one complains of another's aggression, parents do a disservice when they say, "Hit him back!" Picture the scene. Mamma and a friend are having coffee in the kitchen. Her children are outside playing with others of the neighborhood and all is peaceful. Very soon in runs Johnny, crying, upset. "James knocked me down and hit me," he says between sobs. "And what did you do to him?" Mamma says. (Why do we constantly ask children such questions when we know the times are rare when they'll confess?) Naturally Johnny answers, "Nothing." "Well, don't come running to me. Hit him back." The child leaves, realizing he is not going to get much help from his mother except words. If he is a small, timid child, chances are he will not be able to follow his mother's advice, especially if the other child is bigger and more daring. If Johnny is fairly self-reliant already and hits easily, the advice simply means to continue hitting. That will not be of much help either, at least to his reputation.

What the parent really means when he or she says to hit him back is, "You try to learn to cope with your own social problems, take care of yourself and don't keep running to me." Naturally, parents want their children to grow in self-reliance. But I don't believe the hit-him-back formula is the best way to foster this growth. Because when we say this to a child we are suggesting only *one* course of action in a difficult and sometimes complex situation—and that one way is to hit. There are many possible ways for children to cope socially. Give them the opportunity to find their own way. Do not restrict them by ordering just one response.

Just watch a resourceful, imaginative child tackle a difficult situation. He or she suggests, speaks up sternly, distracts the aggressor, or may even cajole, "Stop that or I won't be your friend!" The child may use the very effective threat, "If you don't stop I won't invite you to my birthday party!" even though the birthday is many months away.

At other times, hitting may be just the perfect response for a child in trouble with another. I have seen timid children who have been having a hard time asserting reach the point when they are ready to hit back, and it is the consummate solution. But they must come to this on their own. They cannot respond to being told.

It All Takes Time

Unless the parent is an eyewitness, he or she does not really know what is happening. Has Johnny been pinching James surreptitiously, then screaming self-righteously when James retaliates? And then has Johnny hit back ferociously, acting as if he had been wronged? One year I had a little boy in my class who terrorized the whole group and stood firm upon his high moral plateau with, "My mother told me to hit back." That can put a teacher in a difficult position.

Rather than the automatic response to a child in trouble of "Hit him back," it is far better for the adult to suggest, "See if you and James can talk about your problem. Try to work things out." Or when the child complains of being hit you might respond, "I'm sorry. Don't let him do that to you." When we say these sorts of things we support the child's efforts, but we do not recommend hitting as the only method of coping. Let the child choose an alternative way on the basis of what is comfortable at a particular time and in keeping with his or her nature. When we interfere too soon and too often in children's altercations, we inject the problem with a seriousness it didn't have in the first place. Children's squabbles are usually short-lived when they are allowed to handle them. Friends turn into enemies in a brief moment and flip back to friends just as quickly.

The evolution of social skills does not occur when children are alone too much of the time, when their activities are too closely planned by adults, or when they spend inordinate amounts of time watching television. Young children need ample opportunities in a relaxed and non-judgmental atmosphere to be with others and to experiment with various ways of relating, communicating, and enjoying the company of peers. Parents and teachers cannot prescribe social patterns for them. However, we can provide examples of positive social behavior in our daily interaction with them and make sure they are given the time in which to find their own way.

Today Is
Tomorrow

Chapter 7

IT would be simple if raising children could be computerized. If there were a program for each individual born and all we had to do as parents and teachers was to follow it, there would be no need for questions, doubts, decisions. There would be no opportunity for mistakes; no controversy between child development professionals and psychologists. And no need for books such as this one. We would miss a lot of fun, too. Children and adults would become numbers, and the computer the benevolent authority. It *would* be simple, but fortunately—oh, so very fortunately—this is not the way it is. Human beings cannot be computerized.

Even Adam and Eve in the Garden of Eden could not resist picking the fruit of the tree of knowledge. Though this story indicates that their punishment for disobedience was rejection from paradise and condemnation to the wilderness, I look upon their departure from the garden as their beginning, a challenge to them as individuals of moral capability. Until this act they were not fully human, unable to participate in the decisions and responsibilities from which rise the joys and sorrows of the human condition. I like to think of the fruit of that tree as symbolic of the human capacity for making choices. It could be Randy's bubble gum. Or Jerry's blankelee.

As I conclude this small book, I hasten to note that it is not intended as a scholarly work, but rather a collection of my experiences and insights, disciplined by my profession and influenced by my own childhood and parenthood. As a parent and teacher I am fascinated by the importance of developing the decision-making capabilities of young children. These capabilities are their foundation for the growth of reason, judgment, creativity, and of the utmost importance, their self-esteem and ability to formulate values. My observations have convinced me that we, as parents and teachers, should be considerably more aware of the benefits of encouraging young children to make decisions, to take the initiative, and to assume the responsibility for that initiative. So often when children are small and the decisions within their childish world are minor, we conclude that those decisions do not much matter. From the adult perspective the choices are insignificant— the red dress or the green—so we decide, "Wear the green dress today." And we lay it out. We do not realize that it is the *process* of deciding that encourages competence, not the choice itself, not the color of the dress. We simply do not recognize exactly where and when we may give the youngster opportunities for deciding between alternatives. In this book I have attempted to point out some of these opportunities and to define appropriate areas that may be turned over to the child for his or her determination, with no adult strings attached.

From the time I began this compilation of anecdotes and suggestions for parents and teachers, I have tested the ideas of the preceding chapters in the classroom and through my observations of children wherever I meet them. (I have also raised Randy's allowance once and increased the price of bubble gum in keeping with the changing times.) The evolution of this book reminds me of one of those farmhouses one visits occasionally, where the larger house is built upon and around a cabin dating back many years—a modern kitchen installed around the old wide-hearth fireplace, a wing of several bedrooms to the west built years before that, a veranda to the front added during a different era. If one descends the steep stairs to the dark, cool basement below the primary structure, one can find the sturdy handhewn beams of the original building.

Just as there are some times for the child to decide and others for adult authority, there are some decision-making areas for both to work in together. These cooperative fields are perhaps the most difficult to perceive and to manage. Sometimes they may involve problems of choice that can be negotiated through discussion. These may include daily routines, household and school rules, and parental decisions tempered with a measure of flexibility. It is possible to make sure that children do what we have decided they must do by allowing a bit of leeway, a bit of extra time, a bit of humor, occasionally some bargaining, and a wise allowance for face saving.

We need to remember that children are small beings in a large and often confusing world; they are dependent upon the adults in their lives for direction, approval, and love, but they also need to assert their independence. The tension between dependence and independence runs constantly throughout childhood and peaks in the two-year-old, the four-year-old, and the teenager. While we make our necessary demands, we must recognize the need for what I choose to call face saving. I do not consider this a bad practice when applied to young children, though this same need for face saving in adults may indicate insecurity and immaturity. What a child's need for face saving means is simply the desire for some elbow room in which to rectify an error, change course, or do a chore that is required without sacrificing dignity and self-worth. It is a good idea to let the child take the lead whenever possible, for instance, Sally has dropped her apron on the floor after painting. The teacher says, "Sally, you forgot something." Sally looks around. The teacher continues, "Can you figure out what you forgot?" Sally does, and smiles and picks up the apron agreeably. If the teacher had faulted Sally and demanded harshly that she pick up the apron, Sally may well have balked.

Sammy is busy with his rock collection. He had forgotten to make his bed. Mother reminds, "Sammy, you forgot your bed. Would you like to make it now, or would you rather wait until you come to a good stopping place?" Sammy has no choice about bed making, but he does have leeway as to the timing of the chore. These are small choices within boundaries that we allow children; they are negotiable, and they build a sense of freedom within the requirements of daily life.

Legitimate choices for children are included in a whole host of areas that I have discussed in this book. It must not be forgotten, though, that young children depend on parents and teachers to make the really major decisions with a steady and non-judgmental attitude.

There has been talk recently by some child development professionals that what we do or do not do with our children does not matter as much as we think it does. These ideas are significant and valuable in that they may prevent some of the guilt that develops in parents who have attempted to raise their children "by the book" and after doing everything they are told to do, find the results were not what they were led to expect. Just as we cannot program our children, neither are we entirely responsible for the direction of their growth. Every individual is born with a certain genetic inheritance, and beyond the influence of the home he or she is a product of society, as well. As parents and teachers we are fallible; our mistakes and inadequacies are to be expected. Those experts who are telling us not to worry so much point out that children have a resiliency and toughness that we sometimes do not realize. We can interpret this to mean that when we do our best, follow reasonable guidelines and warmly care about our children, we should not heap excessive blame upon ourselves when things go awry.

On the other hand, the experts who caution against our assumption of an overload of accountability for what happens to a child may encourage a kind of *laissez-faire* attitude in parents: "It doesn't matter what we do with our children, their pattern of growth is determined." The far-reaching effects of that attitude with its invitation to neglect human nurturing is unsettling, to say the least. Because some children who have been subjected in childhood to all kinds of devastating experiences grow into responsible, thinking, emotionally healthy adults, there is no reason to conclude that early experiences do not influence the development of most. That there are some tough children who come through a childhood of hell unscathed is a testament to the invulnerability possible in the human spirit. It is a humbling reminder to all of us who work with children that there are a lot of answers we do not have, and that human beings and human relationships are just tremendously complex.

It would be a violation of our humanity if we were to conclude from these exceptional cases that our thoughtful efforts as parents and early childhood educators do not count. It is my experience and the experience of many others—parents and professionals alike—that how we treat children and how we feel toward them does make a difference.

Rooted in the experiences of early childhood are the values individuals will carve for themselves in later years, their capacity to live according to these values, and their attitudes toward themselves and the human community. Though children are glued to the immediate, their lives circling the present, the way they learn and grow points to what they will become. Today is tomorrow. As little Paula said one morning as she dashed in the classroom door grinning happily, "See, here I am. I told you I would come back tomorrow."